T0380405

ETHICS & CORRUPTION

An Introduction.

About the Author

Vinayan Janardhanan is a career Civil Servant in the Indian Government with over 27 years' experience in Administration, Rail and Aviation operations, Construction, Project Management, Ethical Oversight and Vigilance. He has professional qualifications in Civil Engineering, Marketing Management and Cyber Laws and decades of hands-on experience in the 'sensitive' functions of public procurements, tendering, contract and projects monitoring, He has completed his Doctoral Thesis work from the Indian Institute of Management, Indore in the domain of Anticorruption and Ethics in the OB Area, and received the 'Fellow in Management-Industry' Doctoral Diploma in 2016. He currently works on a Deputation from the Indian Railway Traffic Service with a Public Sector Enterprise in South India as Chief Vigilance Officer. He is a recipient of the National Award for Outstanding Service of the Government of India, Ministry of Railways in 2008. He is married to Swapna, a Psychologist and has two teenaged children – Viswajeet and Sauparnika, and lives in Kochi.

Armed with deep insights from more than a quarter century in senior Public Sector service, and years of passionate research into the vexing phenomenon of Corruption, the Author presents a scholarly, yet lucid 360-degree review on the topic for serious students of the subject and practitioners of Ethical Oversight and Vigilance. Merging the hither-to separately explored streams of Ethics and Corruption research, the Author builds a case for a holistic, multidisciplinary, and most importantly, diagnostic and preventive outlook on Corruption.

ETHICS & CORRUPTION
An Introduction.

A Definitive Work on Corruption
for First-Time Scholars

Vinayan Janardhanan

PARTRIDGE

ISBN: Hardcover   978-1-4828-8410-4
             Softcover   978-1-4828-8408-1
             eBook   978-1-4828-8409-8

Print information available on the last page.

To order additional copies of this book, contact
Partridge India
000 800 10062 62
orders.india@partridgepublishing.com

www.partridgepublishing.com/india

Contents

Dedication

To
Our Parents and Teachers for making Everything possible;
&
Swapna, Viswajeet & Sauparnika
My biggest strengths; and biggest weaknesses!
I love you!

Dedication

Author's Note

This book is drawn from the learnings during the four years' Doctoral study with the Indian Institute of Management, Indore, and also from my twenty seven years of work experience in a variety of sensitive functions in the Government of India. The first realization I had when I started my research work was how little of academic scrutiny has gone into such a pressing - and distressing - phenomenon as corruption, particularly in the Indian context. What we have is a lot of hype and sensationalism with scarce amounts of objectivity and neutrality, leave alone academic rigor.

Corruption, for a scholar, is clearly an area of human behavior that needs to be approached with the same detached and dispassionate interest as for any other field of intellectual enquiry. This is a time when Governments all over the world are beginning to realize the depth behind the pithy quote from the late Dr APJ Abdul Kalam, the former, much-loved Scientist-President of India, "Only three persons can rid the country of its corruption – the Father, the Mother and the Teacher". This book therefore is an aid to the latter, who struggles to find the apt material for the right inputs in the all-important topics of Ethics and Corruption to undergraduate, postgraduate and professional courses. The urgent need for 'Catching Them Young' and for incorporating these topics as subjects to be taught formally in educational institutions is being understood all over the world, and this book is an effort to present some inputs for young adult scholars and their teachers. Along with this, this work also presents for the general readers, a useful source of interesting insights and information on this all-pervasive, yet somewhat mysterious aspect of human behavior.

I acknowledge with deep gratitude all the Authors and Researchers who I have quoted in my work. You went there first and made it easier for me. You certainly know better! Any errors here are all mine. I thank the Professors at IIM Indore particularly my beloved Guides: Prof. Ranjeet Nambudiri, Prof. Sushanta K. Mishra, Prof. Nobin Thomas; and Prof. Praveen K. Parboteeah from University of Wisconsin-Whitewater, USA; for their unstinting support and guidance. I wish to place on record my gratitude to Mr K V Chowdary, Central Vigilance Commissioner of India, and other officers of CVC and Government of India who have permitted and assisted the conduct of the research related to this book. I am greatly honored to have received kind words of encouragement and endorsement for this humble effort from such luminaries and experts in the areas of Administration, Ethical Oversight and Academics as Mr. N. Vittal, Mr. K V Chowdary, Mr. Sri Kumar, Prof. N. Ravichandran and Prof. Rishikesha T. Krishnan, whose messages follow this page. Gratitude is also due to all my friends and colleagues who supported me in my research and in the preparation of this book. I am particularly indebted to my friends Bobby Nair, Jeby Cherian, Balachandra Iyer, Vinod Kumar, Rakesh Bhatnagar, Ani Justus and Mr. AV Thankappan Nair for their invaluable help and encouragement. I thank all my Teachers from my school days onwards, and my Parents and Family who allowed me so much time and supported me in this endeavor. Lastly I thank God for giving me the opportunity to make this humble contribution to the fight against corruption, perhaps the biggest scourge the world has ever known.

As you can now see, only the pen was mine!

A Preface

By
N. Vittal (IAS)
Former Chairman Public Enterprises Selection board, and
former Central Vigilance Commissioner of India

*

N Vittal, IAS, belonged to the 1960 Batch of the Indian Administrative Service, 'The steel framework of the Indian Government'. He is an eminent and respected public servant with over 40 years of wide experience in several critical posts, including that of The Chairman, Public Enterprises Selection Board of India and of The Chief Vigilance Commissioner of India. Earlier, he was the Secretary of Information Technology Department (1990–1996) and of Telecommunications Department (1993–1994) of the Government of India at critical junctures, initiating path-breaking policies for software technology parks and was deeply involved in shaping the liberalization of the telecom sector. He has spoken and written widely on a large number of topics on governance, including corruption, and is the author of several best-selling books such as Ending Corruption? How to clean up India; and The Red-Tape Guerilla. He is a regular columnist for The Economic Times and the Web magazine Rediff-on-the-Net (www.rediffindia. com). He was also awarded the Padma Bhushan, India's 3rd highest civilian award, in 2012.

*

This book on Corruption and Ethics by J Vinayan, Chief Vigilance Officer of The Fertilisers and Chemicals Travancore Ltd is a welcome and timely addition to the body of academic work on the two aspects of social science which have become increasingly important, significant and relevant in our public lives, especially in recent years. This is true for the whole world today.

The issues of all pervasive corruption, the need for good governance and cleanliness in public life have become the major issues of public concern in practically every sphere of life. The 24/7 media channels and the print media are obsessed with it. This trend can be traced perhaps to the late eighties of the 20th century, starting with the demolition of the Berlin Wall in 1989 and the collapse of the Soviet Union in 1990.

The failure of communism and central planning along with the implied global consensus that in matters economic, the customer is supreme and the market oriented liberalism should prevail, brought into sharp focus the need for the ethical element in business. The issue of corruption in governance was perceived to be not only leading to evils like crony capitalism but also failure of the rule of law. Corruption was perceived to be anti-economic development, anti-national and anti-poor.

In our own country the economic liberalization policies introduced in 1991 by the Narasimha Rao government introduced what has been called the LPG era (Liberalization, Privatization and Globalization). The period afterwards has witnessed a number of *cases* especially in the market place (private sector) starting with the notorious Harshad Mehta *case*, Ketan Parekh *case* and on to some other recent cases.

Internationally this concern about fighting corruption has led to the United Nations adopting the 2003 Anti-Corruption Convention. Shri Vinayan has called his book 'purely an academic effort on corruption and ethics. The target audience is the students of undergraduate, postgraduate and professional colleges.' As he points out, ethics is now being taught is colleges and schools and there is a shortage of material for covering these subjects. Indeed, there is a paucity of serious academic scrutiny or research into corruption which is a monstrous problem in our country.

The author has drawn the contents of this book largely based on his doctoral work on the subject at IIM Indore. Shri Vinayan has displayed by this book a more creative and public spirited imagination to prove the truth of the age old maxim: *'Vidya Viniyogat Vikasite'* [Knowledge spreads by broad casting]. Money gets spent by distribution. Knowledge and wisdom are just the opposite!

I spent more than four decades of my life as a civil servant and based on my experience in the field, I congratulate Dr Vinayan on packing so much of valuable information about such a wide spectrum of aspects relating to corruption and ethics in this handy, reader friendly book.. I am sure that amount of information this book gives will indeed be of immense value to the students who may not have any idea about the multiple dimensions of both corruption and the problems of ethics.

From the students' point of view the chapters have been designed with a great deal of internal coherence and rationale.. As they go through the book they will be like tourists visiting a new territory in the company of a friendly, highly knowledgeable guide.

As a public servant who had to deal with such issues over a period of more than 4 decades, I would like to highlight the following aspects:

1. In the last chapter of the book, the author has made valuable suggestions for further study and research.. I particularly appreciate his suggestion –'As pointed out by Svensson (2006), there is a need to study the differential effects of corruption as an important area for research. For example, some of the Asian Countries have been able to show fast rates of growth while being ranked high (or among the more corrupt nations) in the Transparency International's Corruption Perception Index. Is corruption less harmful in these countries? Or would they have grown faster if corruption had been lower?

2. In the context of the 2014 general elections and the emergence of the Modi Sarkar, the following suggestion he has made becomes particularly significant.

   'While analyzing the culture perspectives on corruption we saw that notably absent from literature ot date is an explicit examination of the possible relationship between national culture (beyond those identified under institutional factors), professed religious beliefs (beyond the Protestant Christian faith), and the level of perceived corruption in a country (Mensah 2014). Some of the few efforts in this direction seen in literature have been mentioned in our discussions, but there is clearly a need for more in depth studies in this area in different cultural contexts.'

3. In addition I will make just one suggestion.

   In my view in the ultimate analysis it is the nature and the values of the individual public servant that determines whether a system will be free of corruption and operate ethically. This calls for ensuring that the right person with the right quality is given the right assignment which is the best guarantee for integrity and good governance. This aspect needs to be further studied and operationalized by evolving suitable methodologies.

Shri Vinayan deserves congratulations on his excellent book. I wish his book all success!

N.Vittal

A Foreword

By

K.V.Chowdary (IRS),
Central Vigilance Commissioner of India

*

Mr. K.V. Chowdary is an Officer of the 1978 batch of Indian Revenue Service. He has been appointed as Central Vigilance Commissioner by a warrant of the Hon'ble President of India dated 6.6.2015 for a term of 4 years from the date of his assuming the charge, 10ᵀʰ June 2015. Before joining the Central Vigilance Commission, he was Advisor to the Department of Revenue on Black Money and Chairman of the Central Board of Direct Taxes of the Indian Government. He has investigated several sensitive and complicated cases during his tenure in the Taxes domain.

He was a member of Indian delegation for conducting negotiations with OECD in Paris in 2004. He was also a member of the Committee constituted by the Hon'ble Finance Minister of India to redraft the Income Tax Act of India. He was a Member of the Committee on Business Process Re-engineering for the IT Dept. He has also represented India in the International Conferences of Heads of Criminal Investigation at Istanbul Turkey in 2013 and in the Hague, Netherlands in 2014.

He has been a regular guest faculty member of National Academy of Direct Taxes, Nagpur, India on variety of topics such as Investigation Assessments of Companies, Assessments of search and seizure cases, Assessments of Trusts and charitable organizations, Transfer Pricing, International Taxation, Vigilance, etc. He was also a guest faculty of OECD for a training program on "Transfer Pricing".

*

It is indeed gratifying to note that Shri Vinayan, the Chief Vigilance Officer of FACT Ltd., Kochi has taken the effort to bring out a book on Corruption and Ethics, Shri Vinayan's effort in bringing out this educative book on the all-important topic of corruption and ethics is laudable. He has been pursuing his Doctoral work at IIM, Indore for the past few years with the approval of the Commission, and I am happy to note that the fruits of his labour are being shared with the youth of the country in the form of this book.

The Central Vigilance Commission has been pursuing its own outreach programmes over the past few years to take the message of anti-corruption to the society at large and the youth in particular. The Commission believes that there should be focus on the young citizens for making them aware of the ill effects of corruption in society from a very young age. Education is the foundation of a morally sound society. Lesson on ethics should be included in the curriculum of schools and colleges. Children should be taught to achieve their goals, through rightful means. Such education has to start from the family and schools. With encouragement from Central Vigilance Commission, the Vigilance Wings of Airports Authority of India and Bharat Petroleum Corporation Ltd., have started the concept of integrity club in

Kendriya Vidyalayas. The Commission has advised adoption of this concept in other schools.

This book immensely helps the age group of late teens and early twenties – the young adults about to enter the world of careers, jobs and business. I am sure that the lecturers and professors in colleges teaching undergraduate, post-graduate and professional colleges also will be happy to use this book as a valuable text and reference tool for their pedagogy in ethics and corruption.

I wish the book, its author Shri Vinayan and the readers all success.

(Shri K.V.Chowdary)
Central Vigilance Commissioner

New Delhi
24th June, 2016

A Few Comments on this Book

By

R. Sri Kumar (IPS)
Former Director General of Police, Karnataka and
former Vigilance Commissioner, CVC.

*

Mr. R Sri Kumar belongs to the Indian Police Service batch of 1973. As an officer in the IPS, he has worked in several key positions in the State as well as Central Government in Law and Order, Vigilance, Traffic and CBI. He also has a depth of administrative and management experience in Public Enterprises, bringing out ground-breaking reforms and turn-arounds in the Karnataka State Road Transport Corporation and the Karnataka State Police Housing Corporation.

His accomplishments in police service include setting up the country's first cybercrime police station in Bangalore and obtaining ISO qualification for the same, environmental and green building certification for the Karnataka State Police Housing Corporation and playing a vital role in the successful investigations of many crimes of interstate and international ramifications. He is also known for using technology to crack some of the most high-profile cases like the assassination of former Prime Minister Rajiv Gandhi, the 1992 Harshad Mehta scam and the Abdul Karim Telgi fake stamp paper scam.

In 2010, he became Vigilance Commissioner at the Central Vigilance Commission where he had actively advocated mobile computing for filing complaints about corruption through Project Vig-eye, launched by the Central Vigilance Commission with the objective of empowering citizens to report corruption in their neighbourhood.

Mr. Sri Kumar has been decorated with the Indian Police Medal for meritorious service (1989) and President's Police Medal for distinguished services (1995). He has been bestowed the distinguished alumnus award of Indian Institute of Technology, Madras in January 2010. He has also worked as the Chairman of Task Force on Internal Security, Confederation of Indian Industry, Southern Region, and as a social entrepreneur by launching a public charitable Trust called Indian Centre for Social Transformation.

*

My Congratulations to Vinayan on a book well-structured and presented!

When we look at the phenomenon of organizational corruption, we find that certain organisations are notorious for inducting its new recruits quickly into a culture of corruption. This is because the organisation is a *corrupt organisation and not an organisation of corrupt individuals*. Obviously, when the number of corrupt individuals in an organisation, increases beyond a threshold value or when the top management starts showing these tendencies, the organization is not simply one composed of corrupt individuals (OCI) but has turned into a corrupt organization (CO). The time has come then to demolish and start rebuilding a new organisation.

What are the reasons for the existence of organized corruption in an organisation or what gives rise to the fact that private greed always comes before public interest in one organisation and not the other? Could it be that the pathological behaviors of the manager or other staff members in that organisation, - by their manipulative, unethical, shallow and parasitic actions, staff bullying and a desire for power and control - make it a corrupt organisation as compared to another where these traits are predominantly invisible?

Answers to these and other interesting questions are to be found in this treatise by Dr Vinayan. From the exhaustive study which earned his doctoral thesis and the good understanding of the myriad theories of Corruption from such diverse fields as economics, behavioral theory, history, political sciences, psychology and other social sciences, the Author has drawn our attention to several nuggets of information contained in a large catalogue of references, he has so meticulously compiled. It amazes one to notice the range and depth of study and the precise correlations that the author has drawn from the previous treatises on a complex subject of Corruption in public service.

A new term- Corruptance: has been defined by the author as the assessed vulnerability of the systems and procedures of an organization to the risk of corruption; or lack of preparedness of the systems and procedures to the threat of internal corrupt activity.

Awareness of the Ethics Code, presence and action of Ethical Leadership and Inclusion of employees in Ethical decision making have been highlighted by the Author for creating an ethical climate in an organisation. Three resultant paradigms (oft recommended by several other authors) namely Organizational Commitment, Organizational Citizenship Behavior and Quality of Work has been improved upon by the Author by adding 'Transparency', 'Accountability' and 'Deterrence'. These with Technology in my opinion, are to be considered as core parameters to (prevention of) unethical acts including corruption in any Organization.

Only with a sound understanding of the theoretical knowledge about corruptance one can measure the extent of corruptance fairly accurately, and then lay down a successful strategy to combat the same. Any transformation or initiation of reforms in the organization has to flow from the full understanding of the complexity of corruption.

While attempting to write a book on a difficult subject distinct from the already available ones, the author has pointedly identified that it is important to analyze the prevalent systems and processes of an organization *beforehand*. Only by doing so, one can predict the areas vulnerable for corrupt practices within the organization, where timely preventive actions can to be taken. The Vigilance functionaries in an organisation are expected to keep a constant watch on the goings on in the organisation to red flag the indicators that signify the increase of corruptance in an organisation. These conscience keepers are then to suggest ways and means to counter the increasing corruptance and stabilize the organisation before the decay crosses the limits of public tolerance. For the functionaries tasked with such an onerous job, this book can definitely serve as a good reference book or ready reckoner.

The question that troubles me is, with this theoretical knowledge, can one easily devise a methodology to avoid corruption in say a regulatory or watch dog agency? These are the organisations that need to be robust enough to take the leadership of Vigilance management and the challenge of combating the corrupt.

'Fence eating the crop' is an adage in many of the Indian languages. But that does not answer the question, why the head of an organisation charged with the responsibility for weeding out corruption, face not only accusations of being corrupt, but these accusations actually get proved by independent investigations, notwithstanding vociferous denials by the very persons who were selected to hold these sensitive posts? Why did these functionaries not accept moral responsibility and offer to step down when the allegations first surfaced? After all, are they not expected to lead by example?

Where are morality and ethics, and leadership? Ethical leadership is of crucial importance in curbing corrupt practices in an organisation where managers should serve as role models and the company's anti-corruption policies gets communicated and supported from top down

Organizational culture consists of a set of shared meanings, assumptions, values and norms that guide employees' behavior within an organization via explicit structures and conventions. The ethical tone or climate is set at the top. What top management do, and the culture they establish and reinforce, makes a big difference between a corrupt organisation and an organisation of corrupt individuals.

To further improve readability, I would recommend that too many abbreviations be avoided. Impressive list of references and extensive quotes of these authors in the book indicates a scholastic approach to the study. A detailed Cross indexing to show what idea has emanated from which reference would be of great value to future scholars and researchers, I agree with the author that the subject requires continuous study and further research before a dent is made in the fight against the corrupt. My Best Wishes!

R.Sri Kumar
Bangalore
July 2016

A Word for the Academia

By
Dr N. Ravichandran
Senior Professor, IIM Ahmedabad and former Director of IIM, Indore.

*

Prof. Dr N. Ravichandran is one of the most accomplished academicians of India in the Management Education domain. Currently at the Indian Institute of Management, Ahmedabad, he was the Director of the Indian Institute of Management Indore for several years where he was credited with the rapid creation of world-class infrastructure at this newly created Institute, starting the popular five-year Integrated Management Programme, increasing the batch size of the flagship PGP programme from 240 to 450 and introducing the PGP at RAK in the UAE and at Mumbai.

An educationist par excellence, he is an MSc in Maths a holds a PhD from the Indian Institute of Technology, Madras. He teaches Operations Management and Quantitative Techniques, and has authored more than 50 research papers in his areas of research. His areas of interest include Information Technology Strategy, Competitiveness, Operations Management, Quantitative Methods, Applied Simulation and Stochastic Processes and their applications. His current research includes Stochastic Models in Management Science and Management Information Systems.

Besides his commitments with the premier Indian Management Institutes, he also Consults and has been a visiting faculty to many academic institutions in Europe and India.

*

I am happy to note that Mr. Vinayan, who obtained his Ph.D. from IIM, Indore recently has enlarged his thesis as a book. This book is both relevant and timely to our country.

As a nation we have moved far away from the statement that corruption is a global phenomenon to a government which wants to eliminate corruption from all walks of life on a priority basis.

Unlike many other countries, India is endowed with abundant natural resources, talent manpower, large domestic market and an young population to accomplish its growth agenda. What has been possibly holding us in the last 70 years since independence in meeting completely the aspirations of our people, government and community is corruption and lack of transparency in Public life.

It is not necessary to elaborate on the negative impact of corruption in public/private spending. What is needed is to discourage inappropriate practices under control by continuous surveillance, rapid administrative corrective action on reported incidents and a change in the mindset at all level from common citizens to the highest authority of the land to prevent corruption and promote transparency in public life and public spending.

It is well known for a variety of reasons; our academic institutions have not distinguished themselves by exemplary research. When it comes to research leading to meaningful insights of socially relevant issues, the reported research is still sparse. This situation is expected to change shortly. It is in this context, the volume under consideration is a welcome addition.

I am sure, this book promotes awareness related to prevention of corruption and enable people to discuss, debate, propagate social mechanisms to create a corruption free India.

Ahmedabad
8 September 2016   N. Ravichandran

A Noteworthy and Exemplary Effort

By
Prof. Rishikesha T Krishnan
Director, IIM Indore, India.

*

Rishikesha T. Krishnan is Director and Professor of Strategic Management at the Indian Institute of Management Indore, India. Prior to this, he was a member of the faculty at the Indian Institute of Management, Bangalore (IIMB), India.

Professor Krishnan has been a Visiting Scholar at the Center for the Advanced Study of India, University of Pennsylvania, and at the Indian School of Business, Hyderabad. He held the Jamuna Raghavan Chair in Entrepreneurship at IIMB from 2007-10.

Professor Krishnan's main areas of interest are strategy and innovation. He was listed among the Thinkers50 India most influential thinkers in management from India (2013) and jointly received the special Thinkers50 India Innovation award (2013). Earlier, he received the Dewang Mehta Award for Best Teacher in Strategic Management in 2010.

Professor Krishnan's recent book, 8 Steps to Innovation: Going from Jugaad to Excellence *(co-authored with Vinay Dabholkar, and published by Harper Collins in March 2013), outlines a systematic path for organizations to build innovation capabilities. This book has been chosen as the Best Book of 2013-14 by the Indian Society for Training and Development.*

Professor Krishnan is an alumnus of IIT Kanpur, Stanford University and IIM Ahmedabad.

*

It was with considerable interest that I went through this book, borne out of the Author's Doctoral Research at IIM-Indore.

This work is noteworthy on several counts. For one, the *raison d'etre* for the book is rooted in hardcore practical experience and problems faced by practitioners of Ethical Oversight and Vigilance across the world; and this community is surely going to be benefited by these insights. Secondly, the author has managed to present a lucid and reader friendly discussion on such a complicated and vexing socio-economic problem as corruption, combining real- life corruption case data with robust academic research. Third is the intention behind the book: to present a 360 degree analysis of the topic directed towards students, researchers and practitioners, besides serious general readers.

The logical sequencing of the chapters and the abundance of perspectives, all thickly foot noted, make this book a valuable reference guide. The special chapter on India and the suggested Principles of Public Integrity are interesting and inspirational. IIM Indore has been laying special emphasis on scholar – practitioner streams of research and Vinayan's effort is an exemplary product of the unique practitioner-focused doctoral programme of our Institute.

I commend Vinayan for this effort and wish the book all success.

Rishikesha T Krishnan
Indian Institute of Management, Indore.
September, 2016.

Chapter I

Introduction and the Need for this book

*

This Chapter presents broadly the vision and mission of this work. The overview of the book and the different chapters, the research questions set out to begin the study, and the aims sought to be achieved by the close of this book – all of them from a preventive and defensive point of view against corruption – are presented here.

*

"Today, all our day-to-day activities are
managed by organizations."

At its core, this book is about Organizational Corruption (OC). The human civilization evolves through its societies. All our day-to-day activities and the works of longer duration today - be it business, recreation, academics, research or religion - are managed not by individuals, but by organizations. In fact, our continually evolving societies are no longer best described as societies of *individuals,* but rather as societies of *organizations;* and the modern business organization, including governmental, non-governmental and religious organizations, has now achieved societal dominance (Gioia, 2003). This is true even for the most recent and popular Internet forums for personal interaction between people – the ubiquitous social media, the smart phone applications and the chat rooms where individuals or small groups carry on their private conversations. When we stand back and look at these platforms dispassionately, though the ground level interactions involve just two or a few persons, actually it is organizations are what are running these forums. The content providers, the Internet service providers, the data centers housing the servers that host these programs, the software developers, the hardware suppliers and managers, the security, advertising and marketing departments, the research and development teams or organizations and so on. Also, whether we know it or like it there are whole crowds of organizations monitoring, assessing, and even controlling the traffic in these modern communication channels and forums. Often organizations themselves participate in and direct the course these conversations take, for a variety of reasons. We see therefore, that this is also organizational business, as usual. This brings the study of organization right to the forefront in the next wave of societal thinking. In most economies, particularly those of the Developing Economies like India and her neighbors, governmental organizations and State-Owned Enterprises (SOEs) still manage substantial assets on behalf of their people, though the role of governments in running their own business organizations is gradually slackening, as part of the ongoing wave of globalization, liberalization and privatization. With the role and impact of business organizations becoming all-pervasive, the global fight against corruption is also bringing its focus to bear on an *organizational* perspective towards the phenomenon of corruption. An act of corruption performed within the environment of the organization could have much more impact on society, economy and common good than one happening in transactions between individuals outside it. This book seeks to present a collated set of material for first-time scholars of Ethics and Corruption through an extensive review of extant literature on Organizational Corruption, synthesis of the same taking into account multi-disciplinary perspectives and theories; antecedents and effects of corruption; currently available tools with practitioners and in theory for measuring corruption and suggest certain new directions for research. This book also proposes to extend discussion on *precursors, mediators and moderators* of OC, which are comparatively less discussed aspects of OC. Finally this book proposes the concept of *Corruptance* of Organizations (discussed below).

At the outset we make four assumptions: *One*; The entire discussion in this book will be on Organizational Corruption (OC) or Corruption in the Organizational Context (COC), and we will use the terms Corruption, OC and COC interchangeably. *Two*; COC refers to the behavior of individuals or groups or the organization as a whole, all *within the organizational setting*. This means that acts of corruption performed between two individuals or groups *outside* an organizational context are outside our ambit. *Three*; by *Organization* we mean the modern formal private and public business organizations including any Governmental organization such as a Public (State-owned Enterprise) or a governmental department engaging in business transactions. This therefore excludes individual behavior outside of the organizational setting, non-business activities of NGOs, religious organizations etc. *Four*; we assume that corruption in any form is not good for society or common good and needs to be prevented or eradicated.

Corruption in the Organizational Context (COC) or Organizational Corruption (OC) is highly undesirable for any parties holding a stake in the organization's performance (Lange, 2008). An *organizational* perspective towards corruption is important because, like all other societal phenomena, an organization has evolved a basic unit in the practice of corruption also (Luo, 2004). COC can be considered as *the furthering of individual interests by one or more organizational actors through the intentional misdirection of organizational resources or perversion of organizational routines, this behavior being ostensibly on behalf of the corporation rather than against it* (Lange, 2008). Most corrupt activities, from a *macro* perspective, take place between profit-driven organizations (on the supply side) and government officials, legislators or other organizations (on the demand side). There are also numerous examples of corrupt activities performed by individuals, groups or the organization itself against other individuals, organizations or the general public or national exchequer. In the backdrop of the numerous scams that shook the economies of many countries in the early years of this millennium, Ashforth et al (2008) highlight the need to focus on *corruption* in the organizational context, as against the somewhat related (but different) notions such as *unethical behavior, antisocial behavior, dysfunctional deviance, organizational misbehavior, counter-productive work behavior* etc., which are also located within the organizational setting. We will be analyzing all these concepts in the course of this book. Corruption, unlike these others, is a strong and provocative term implying a willful perversion of order, ideals and trust (Ashforth et al, 2008) and in the organizational context, has been becoming a grave matter for concern afflicting *everything*, for-profit, not-for-profit, governmental, and even religious organizations; and being displayed not only by individuals in organizations, but by organizations themselves (Ashforth et al, 2008).

"Pressing Need for a 360-degree
look at the phenomenon"

In the last two decades, researchers have begun to look with increasing intensity at the phenomenon of Corruption. The need for a focused look at Corruption in organizations stems from the following three facts. *One,* the current management literature is atomized in that existing models of negative organizational behaviors like Corruption focus mainly on *static individual* traits and behaviors and the individual, interpersonal, and group level factors that influence them. (Ashforth et al, 2008). The resulting views presented by scholars of Corruption are relatively narrow leading to a relative neglect of the *role of processes and systems* (Brass, Butterfield & Skaggs 1998). A systemic view is obviously important because corruption appears to thrive in particular organization, industry, and national environments (Ashforth et al, 2008), and we need to examine just what is different about these environments. There is a need to juxtapose organizational corruption against the other organizational misconducts/misbehaviors in the backdrop of the organizational systems and processes on one hand; and culture, norms and practices on the other. Such a 360-degree relook must also examine the COC phenomenon from the perspectives of other disciplines such as psychology, sociology, anthropology, economics, law, political science as well as organizational behaviour. One of the aims of this book is to conceptualize the above *context* of Organizational Corruption, for the benefit of the serious student of the domain.

Two, for controlling or eliminating Corruption we first need to have a truly *integrative, interactive and processual* understanding of Corruption in organizations (Ashforth et al, 2008). Therefore, there is a need to study closely and simultaneously the organizational *antecedents* shaping corruption from the micro-, meso- and macro- perspectives, the *precursors* or 'warning bells' to corruption, the organizational *systems, processes* and *behaviors* permitting, rationalizing and reflecting corruption, its *mediators* and *moderators*, and the *consequences* generated by corruption. The next domain which needs to be surveyed is that of *measurement* of corruption (or of corruption *perception*, which is what is actually measured today), and the efforts at various levels for *controlling* Corruption, as seen from literature as well as from practitioners. In this book we will examine each of these facets of Corruption.

Three, we assume that elimination of COC is a *sine qua non* for achieving the larger social good of all. The common - often unspoken- purpose behind all research and study in organizational behavior is for suggesting ways of managing organizations to the overall benefit of the society and as instruments for creating 'common' wealth, over and above personal and organizational wealth (from Ashforth et al 2008, Gioia, 2003a). We all understand that 'prevention is better than cure', and thus there is a pressing need to focus our efforts on trying to predict, and where possible, prevent the possibility of Corruption and unethical behavior occurring in organizations. In this we look at the antecedents as well as effects of COC from this perspective of *preventing* organizations from becoming vulnerable to corruption. Misangyi, Weaver and Elms (2008) argue that the getting rid of institutionalized corruption requires changes in both the symbolism and substance of corrupt institutional systems through development of non-corrupt routines rooted in newly constructed frameworks with a specific purpose. We propose the term 'Corruptance' to mean the perceived and assessed vulnerability of the systems and procedures of the organization to the risk of corruption; or lack of preparedness of the systems and procedures to the threat of internal corrupt activity. Later, we will go on to propose the concept of a Corruptance Index for organizations to indicate an aggregate assessed value of the structural and procedural lacunae or lack of preparedness of the organization in preventing misuse or abuse of the systems and procedures through these lacunae, which provide an environment conducive for corruption to flourish. The Corruptance Index for organizations will be different from the existing Corruption Indexes like Corruption Perception Index (Transparency International), Control of Corruption Indicator (World Bank) etc. in that the latter are all perception-based, assessed at country-levels and from ex-post perspectives while the Corruptance Index is derived from the specific structural and procedural factors at organizational level and is ex ante and preventive in perspective. We provide the theoretical basis for this future work through this book. The long-term purpose of this work is to prepare the ground for such a new framework and following that the Corruptance Index, for continued research, which will be built on such a comprehensive review and contextualization of COC along with its antecedents, effects and efforts at control of corruption.

*

Ensuing from such a review and synthesis of literature on COC, this book puts forth an agenda for continued research with some specific questions being asked at the beginning of our study. These include, questions such as "Is it possible to derive from theory, certain variables from the structure, and environment of organizations, which can point towards the organization's corruption vulnerability or anticorruption preparedness?" "Is it possible to assess an organization's vulnerability to corruption?; and, "Is it possible to grade and compare multiple organizations' relative preparedness against corruption?" We propose the new term Corruptance to mean the assessed vulnerability of the systems and procedures of the organization to the risk of corruption; or lack of preparedness of the systems and procedures to the threat of internal corrupt activity. As continuing research beyond this book, we will later on attempt to suggest a tool to assess Corruptance of organizations.

*

Chapter II

Perspectives on Corruption

*

For proper appreciation of any socio-economic phenomenon, it is necessary to understand how the phenomenon is observed from various points of view. This chapter examines how Corruption is viewed by various disciplines and streams of research. We look briefly at the perspectives on this phenomenon by the domains of History, Sociology, Political Science, Psychology, Anthropology, Economics, Law, Management Studies, Culture, Religion, etc. We have also collated the various perspectives into three broad streams: Micro, Macro and Mixed perspectives, and presented them in a comprehensive table.

*

History: Fein and Weibler (2014) point out that the scholars of history look at the *dynamics* of the development of various phenomena in history. Historians describe how, with passage of time, the concept of corruption as well as the value system defining what is legitimate and what is corrupt have both changed (Engels, Fahrmeir, & Nutzenadel, 2009). Fein and Weibler (2014) conclude that historians generally interpret corruption as a typical product of modernization, underlining the historical relativity of corruption (Volkov, 2000) and its relationship with the State, a specific type of social organization (Fein, 2014).

"Aristotle"

The historical perspective of corruption generally begins with the thoughts of the three famous thinkers of ancient Greece - of Socrates (469–399 BCE), Plato (427–347 BCE) and Aristotle (384–322 BCE). Though these three philosophers had differences in their thinking there were several parameters common to all three of them in their outlook on corruption. Each of them had a systemic perspective on corruption and saw it as a part and parcel of human relationships including the political association, which was expected to be an epitome of morals and virtues- a Republican ideal. They associated corruption with the abuse of power destroying the moral and political fiber of civil society against the welfare of the republic. They also considered corruption as the decay and destruction of morals and virtue in an attempt to cater to private interests of individuals and groups (O'Hara, 2014).

"Plato"

Mulgan, (2012) points out that history of European philosophy of the late-classical and Hellenistic periods is replete with examples of discussion of corruption in politics and the possibility of achieving non-corrupt politics, from philosophers like Socrates, Plato and their successors. Their biggest worry was about politicians and their corruption. Socrates propounded new philosophies such as Cynicism, Epicureanism and Stoicism as opportunities for quietist withdrawal by politicians from politics. Plato never condemned the realm of politics though he placed it in the lower level in his dualistic universe. Aristotle also re-affirmed his belief that the eternal unchanging realm of intellect reachable only through pure reason was certainly above the sub-lunar world of political change and uncertainty. These philosophers appear to have believed in a kind of ontological dualism where the realm of truth and nobility was placed above a lower world of uncertainty, evil and corruption. Most of these philosophers placed politics in this inferior world. The modern ideas on corruption such as *misuse of public resources for private gain, abuse of power for personal benefit,* etc. can be linked back to the original thoughts of these philosophers. One difference the Greek Philosophers showed in their approach to battling corruption was the ideal that the non-corrupt States are governed by pure and virtuous individuals whose only interest is the common good and place no value at all on their own or private interest. Aristotle was slightly different in that his rulers had their own private lives, but as far as their official or political life was concerned all their acts were exclusively for the good of the republic. Though their concepts were somewhat Utopian, they may be considered to be moral precursors to the modern concepts of pure non-corrupt government.

"Indian Thinkers philosophized on Corruption
thousands of years ago"

In ancient historical periods, Chanakya (or Kautilya) (from L.K.Jha & K.N.Jha, 1998) writes in his *Arthashastra* dated 3rd Century BC, about numerous examples of practices in the society of those days. He described many of the then-common maneuvers such as *pratibandha* (delaying), *prayoga* (money lending), *vyavahara* (insider trading), *avastara* (changed accounting), *pariahapana* (under-collection of taxes), *upabhoga* (misappropriation) and *apahara* (defalcation). He urges the King to be wary of such practices and to take action to control them.

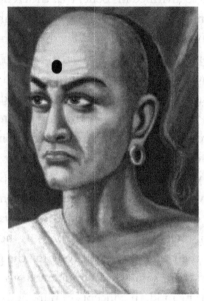

"Chanakya"

Chanakya points out that just as one cannot avoid tasting the honey on the tip of the tongue, the employee of the King cannot avoid taking a bit of the King's resources for himself. Kautilya's observations, coming from the Chief Accountant or Chief Minister of the King, certainly look at the phenomenon from the *'rational-economic man'* lens, where the individual behavior is concerned. Here again Chanakya, like Aristotle, makes no comments about the need for or absence of the same high standards of behavior in the private lives of the king or the Ministers, while attacking the officials' behavior during performing of public duties.

A few centuries later, Kalhana (12th Century AD, Kashmir, India) in his *Rajatarangini* talks about the activities of some of the courtiers around the king and requests the king to stay away from their intent. Kalhana has also cited some examples of the common incidents in the local kingdoms of his time. He said that the *'Bijja'* became even richer than the king as he sought unfair means of making money, while *'Ananda'* managed to achieve a high post in the King's office by getting favors from higher officials. Another author from the same period, Kshemendra (11th Century AD, Kashmir, India) in his *Dasavataracharitam* advises the King to remove all the courtiers and priests from office with immediate effect, who were either seen to be undesirable or unproductive. Yet another work by Kshemendra, called *Narmamala*, depicts some concerns spreading fast and need to be controlled. He also found an answer to the much discussed question of how to prevent such activities in the kingdom; he has explicitly addressed the contemporary intelligentsia to step forward and shoulder this responsibility.

These writings from history show that in those ancient societies, wherever the public and private lives and functions have been segregated, those in power, like the Kings of ancient, were seized of the need to inculcate ethical practices in administration and in society. On the other hand, in these 'pre-modern' societies, the private activities including private businesses were not yet submitted to such scrutiny, which started happening only in modern societies. Fein (2014) reports that Senturia (1930), one of the first modern researchers in this domain, held the view that the understanding of the term 'corruption' depended on the opinion of the respective observer and the dominant political and public morality of that period. Johnston (2005) suggests that we use the concept of corruption to ask questions about state, society and political change, rather than about particular behavior, because corruption is a political and normative concept rather than a kind of natural category of unacceptable action (Fein, 2014). Plumpe (2009) referring to James Cameron Scott's classic work *Comparative Political Corruption* (1972), claims that corruption and modernity are co-evolving phenomena since only modernity has set up extensive judicial rules governing economic life, while common behavior was not regulated before (Fein, 2014).

Perhaps this theory is being substantiated even today in many Developing economies in the wake of the 'globalization-liberalization-privatization' wave sweeping across the world. There is severe resistance, and mal-adjustments to this trend experienced from several countries; and Ashforth et al (2008) suggest from contemporary experience that recently deregulated industries may be particularly susceptible to corruption. As competition increases, the pressure to meet bottom-line demands becomes increasingly intense, especially for public companies. At the same time, external controls that would have applied counter-pressures to toe the legal line have disappeared. Could this be one reason why many of the scandals of the 1990s occurred in financial services, telecommunications, energy, and health care—all industries that had recently been deregulated? (Ashforth et al., 2008).

Economics: For neo-institutionalist authors in the Economics domain (like Rose-Ackerman, 2000) corruption, in its elemental expression, is an *agency* problem that can be modeled through a scheme with three actors whose nucleus is a principal–agent relationship and a third party (customer). The principal (authority, employer, state etc.) delegates the decision-making power and resources to the agent and the agent defrauds the principal and violates rules by giving an illegal gain to the customer and to himself. Consequently, corruption involves the breach of a contractual relationship, both formal and informal, in which the agent receives a payment as a result of the abuse of their power of decision. Most of the time, economists use the notion of corruption as the "use of public office for private gains," and usually take a different approach from the social scientists, emphasizing the need for appropriate incentives and punishments instead of looking at violations of values and ethics (Bardhan, 2006). Bardhan (2006) states that in the case of the use of public office for private gains, there are two general kinds of corruption: (i) bureaucratic corruption, which is what much of the literature is about in economics; and (ii) political corruption. Another major distinction made in the literature is that between "grand" and "petty" corruption. The term grand corruption refers to "high-level" corruption by elected politicians or by higher-level political appointees, the term petty corruption is usually reserved for administrative or lower-level bureaucratic corruption. This differentiation is similar to the "need-based" and "greed-based" corruption espoused by some other scholars. Although this divide had existed very early on in the literature, Susan Rose-Ackerman (1975) was among the first to explicitly lay out the distinction between the two types.

It has been pointed out that much of the literature on corruption in the social sciences, particularly Economics, has restricted itself to the public sector. This is objectionable, for several reasons (Hodgson and Jiang, 2007). It ignores the reality of corruption in the private sphere which is a clear and present fact of life, be it the Enron scam in the West, the Satyam Scam[1] of India, the frauds by FIFA officials in Caribbean football[2] or bribe taking by cricket players in South Africa[3]. In our discussions in this book, we make no such differentiation between the phenomena occurring in private or public organizations.

Sociology: Corruption cannot be seen in isolation from the social environments in which it arises. However, the analysis of the causality of corruption remains a controversial topic in the field of studies on the social determinants of economic activity. (Lo'pez & Santos, 2014). Supporting the New Economic Sociology (NES) perspective, Lopez and Santos (2014) point out that the economic approach to the problem of corruption as propounded by many including Rose-Ackerman (1975, 1978) and others have barely proved effective in the long run. According to the economic approach, the origin of the problem lies in *institutional and organizational* aspects. The agents will succumb to corrupt practices if they have discretion, weak accountability, and a substantial monopoly of power at their disposal. Consequently, reformers could reduce corruption by curtailing this discretion, increasing control over officials and reducing the power of the state. But Lopez and Santos (2014) remind us that evidence shows that individuals develop bureaucracies, corrupt practices, and attitudes conditioned by a broader socioeconomic environment. It is specifically culture, shared values and social networks in which individuals are inserted that influence behavior, the functioning of the economy and the institutional and legal basis (Hofstede, 2003). Moreover, these factors which uphold the framework of society and, by extension, of the economy, and are hard to alter by means of policy actions (Treisman 2000; Paldam 2002). NES, on the other hand affirms that it is inappropriate to consider corruption as the exclusive result of inadequate organizational and institutional framework. This proposal adopts the basic results of the New Institutional Economics (NIE) and its derivatives on Game Theory (transaction costs, probability

---

1   From http://www.thehindu.com/specials/timelines/satyam-scandal-who-what-and-when/article7084878.ece accessed on 14 April 2014.
2   From http://www.independent.co.uk/sport/football/news-and-comment/fifa-corruption-caribbean-football-chiefs-jack-warner-and-jeffrey-webb-took-aid-for-haiti-earthquake-a6759651.html) accessed on 13 January 2016..
3   From http://news.bbc.co.uk/2/hi/sport/cricket/783834.stm accessed on 13 January 2016.

of uncovering etc.) as a starting point, but completes them with an analysis of the cultural roots of corruption (Lo´pez & Santos, 2014). From the NES perspective, the level of corruption in a society is associated with certain forms of trust and norms that materialize in social networks (social capital) and that project an evaluative configuration "a priori" about what is socially desirable (culture). In this sense, one would expect the prevalence of cultural models that emphasize social distance or a culture of dependency, coupled with low levels of generalized trust to play an important role in explaining corruption problems (Lo´pez & Santos, 2014).

According to Freisitzer (1981), corruption is an *action that deviates from the general normative expectations, in search for a personal benefit or for the benefit of a restricted group, mainly by misappropriation of a public resource.* Using the classical sociological terminology of Tonnies (1947), Lopez and Santos (2014) contrast two extreme models of society: a *cold* society and a *warm* society. In the first type there are no relations between individuals and therefore interpersonal knowledge is very limited, even within families. In contrast, a warm society implies the existence of an extensive network of personal relationships and mutual knowledge. In these societies, family contacts are extremely frequent and the family is a strong network of mutual aid. Purely 'economical' relations as suggested by the Economics perspective are more likely to be found within the context of a cold society, while social distance could be even considered as unacceptable in a warm one. The sociology perspective reminds us that the kinds of relationships envisaged in the 'rational/economical' explanation of corruption are socially conditioned. Lopez and Santos (2014) emphasize that to explain the extent of corruption in a given economy it is necessary to consider the legal system, the dimension of the state and the instruments managed by the authorities to achieve their objectives. However, the persistence of the problem in the long run seems associated with socio-cultural factors. A particular configuration of the cultural dimensions and social networks will limit the impartiality of public actions and the ability to punish or prevent corruption.

Fein & Weibler (2014) highlight several instances to show that the same patterns of behavior, today commonly evaluated as 'corrupt' can be seen to have existed as normal, if not accepted, practices in developing or modernizing countries as in the case of historical pre-modern societies. They cite from previous researchers (Arlacchi, 1989; Voslensky, 1987; Scott, 1985) the examples of the Italian mafia, the socialist systems such as the erstwhile Soviet Union and even the "proto-corruption" that prevailed in 17th / 18th century England. Sociologists also found that whether or to what extent corrupt behavior comes to be critically reflected depends to a large extent on variables of education and social development.

We can therefore see that, like the historical perspectives, sociological view-points also treat Corruption as phenomenon of perception, based on perspectives of those who analyze it (von Alemann, 2005).

"Anthropology: From the perspective of
the acting individual"

Anthropology: Anthropological studies also seem to complement the findings of the above analysis of Sociological and Historical perspectives (Fein, 2014). Anthropology, in the context of corruption, is concerned with micro-level behavioral practices such as *reciprocity* with regard to their social function as central principles of human communication, and thereby as means of establishing relations of mutual trust (Mauss, 2002). From this micro perspective, the predominant explanation for corruption resides in the *attributes of individuals or small groups of colluding individuals*. At a basic level, scholars have used demographic information to attempt to predict corrupt behavior, though without much success, reports Ashforth et al., (2008). However, Anthropology focuses on the perspective of the acting individuals themselves and hence this is a unique contribution different from other streams. Anthropology also studies the

15

self-perception of corrupt individuals and explains in what way social relations are related to individual and collective though processes and also how the methods of assessing change with changing social norms and identities. Anthropology also warns us that making value judgments too strongly can inhibit a proper analysis of the logic of behavior and the relationship established (Fein, 2014).

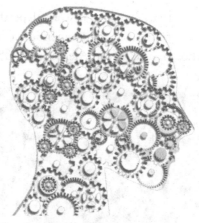

"Individual Predispositions"

Psychology: While use of demographic and anthropological studies to predict unethical behavior have met with limited success, somewhat more reliable results have been reported with study of *individual predispositions* like lack of integrity, empathy, self-control or moral identity or low levels of cognitive moral development or diagnosable psychopathology. This internal locus of attribution suggests that corruption can be eliminated if only organizations can root out and keep out corrupt individuals (Lanyon & Goodstein, 2004). Psychological research has made important contributions to our understanding of corrupt behavior focusing, for example, on motives of bribe-taking (Richter, 1989). Ashforth et al (2008) point out that there is research contending that the seeds of corruption rest not in individual predispositions but in the more generalized limits of human cognitive capability and information processing capacity; and that in these views, corrupt practices have been explained by the failure to recognize the moral nature of situations (Butterfield, Trevino & Weaver, 2000; Jones, 1991; Reynolds, 2006; Werhane, 1999) and the routine operation of systematic cognitive biases (Banaji, Bazerman & Chugh, 2003; Messick & Bazerman, 1996; Moore, Tetlock, Tanlu & Bazerman, 2006), as well as human tendencies to disengage moral standards (Bandura, 1986,

1999), reframe behavior via rationalizing ideologies (Ashforth & Anand, 2003; Robinson & Kraatz, 1998), and use of cognitive scripts that tend to exclude ethical dimensions (Gioia, 1992). In other words, some people embarking upon or indulging in corruption simply may not be able to recognize their acts as being immoral, unethical or corrupt.

Thus we can see that scholars of micro-level perspectives such as Psychology and Anthropology do give importance to both individual and organizational factors that encourage unethical individual acts. However, the micro perspective does not look at the corresponding outcome beyond the individual and sub-group levels. Much of the literature in the micro-perspective appears to be confined to individual acts of corruption and its repercussions. This has actually diverted attention from more dynamic, systemic and processual perspectives on organizational corruption (Ashforth et al, 2008).

Culture and Religion: Very few studies are seen in literature analyzing corruption with culture and religion as an explanatory variable. While analyzing of corruption, many scholars have suggested religious beliefs of the individual actor as a possible contributing factor behind the act. But this particular assumption has not been tested much and except in very few instances, most of the available studies in this domain only deal with Protestant Christian Religion as a typical Religion for comparing with others. Temin (1997) defines culture as the distinctive attitudes and actions that differentiate groups of people. Culture in this sense is the result of and expressed through religion, language, institutions, and history. Defined this way, it is easy to see the connection between culture and religion, and how both are related to human behavior (including proclivities to corruption) (Mensah, 2014).

Lipset & Lenz, (2000) highlight two sociological approaches that help illuminate the relationships between culture and corruption. The first stems from the work of Sociology's founding figure Emile Durkheim, as extensively formulated by Robert K Merton. In his *Social Theory and Social Structure*, Merton presents a *means-ends* schema that can account for variations in norm violations. A second relates to *family*. Political scientist Edward Banfield developed an intriguing analysis of the ways in which a strong familial orientation as in southern Italy and Sicily helps explain high levels of corruption. The underlying theory stems from Plato, who pointed out that the inherent relations between family members, especially parents and children, press them to give particular preferences (nepotism). Banfield noted that corruption is linked to the strength of family values involving intense feelings of obligation. Merton's theory implies that cultures that stress economic success as an important goal but nevertheless strongly restrict access to opportunities will have higher levels of corruption (Lipset & Lenz, 2000)

Mensah (2014) undertook meta-analysis with a twofold purpose: One; to examine whether culture exists as a separate explanatory factor for corruption; and two; to investigate whether other religions besides the Protestant Christian faith have a similar anti-corruption effect. Mensah's (2014) results show the relationship (incremental) between culture and religion and perceived corruption. Mensah has controlled for other economic and social factors. Compared to Protestant Christianity; the other players like Islam, Non-Protestant Christianity and No Religion/Other Religion appear to be related to higher corruption or negatively with anticorruption. However, Buddhism and Hinduism are seen to be much more similar to Protestant Christian Religion with regard to corruption. Mensah's study on culture shows that in comparison with the Anglo-Saxon cultural tradition the other European cultures appear to be positively associated with higher corruption, except where there are good systems of effective governance in place such as in the German and Nordic cultures. Mensah's (2014) study suggests that all the non-European cultures are associated with higher corruption except where this is offset by greater political legitimacy or greater political effectiveness. The examples for the former are Latin America, Middle East, Caribbean, etc. and for the latter are Confucian and South East Asian cultures (Mensah, 2014).

Similarly, North et al (2013) examine whether a nation's dominant religious culture affects the rule of law and the degree of control over corruption. They conclude that (i) the rule of law is stronger in countries whose largest religious group in the year 1900 was Protestantism, Catholicism or Hinduism; (ii) corruption is lower in countries whose largest religious group in 1900 was Protestantism; and (iii) rule of law is stronger and corruption is lower in countries whose largest religious group in 2000 was an Asian ethno-religion. There is clearly a need for more, deeper and wider studies along these streams.

Legal Perspective: Anders & Nuijten (2007) inform us that the apparent opposites such as virtue/vice or legal/illegal are not actually opposites mutually exclusive of each other. They are, as Taussig (1999) said, two sides of the same coin or two dimensions of a single co-joined in an ambivalent relationship. Anders & Nuijten (2007) quote Heyman and Smart (1999) to illustrate that the law of the land has, as its side shows, areas of ambiguity and areas of corruption and illegality. Roitman (2005) also highlights the various ways in which the regular economy and the black money economy (illegal) are related to and dependent on each other. The State and its machinery are inextricably mingled with the legal economy on one hand and the illegal economy on the other and apparently are at the heart of both regulated and unregulated economic transactions. The recent revelations (several news reports, 2016) of vast amounts of black money (untaxed, undisclosed in the parent countries) stashed away in 'tax-havens' like Panama and some other countries by celebrities, politicians and businessmen from numerous countries are testimony to this.

Anders & Nuijten, (2007) conclude that corruption is thus at the very core of order inscribed into the law of the nation-state. Organizational corruption, since it lies in close proximity and tenuous relationship with the other side of the coin, is characterized by gossip, rumors, conspiracy and accusations. Therefore, *the secret of law* is that the clear chances for violation, perversion and corruption are already present at the core of law (Anders & Nuijten, 2007).

Organization Studies: The studies mentioned here come under the fields of Organizational Behavior, Behavioral Ethics, Management Studies and to some extent, Behavioral economics. Fein, (2014) have analyzed several recent papers under these domains including Lange (2008), Shadnam & Lawrence (2011), Rabl (2011), von Maravic (2007), Luo (2004) and Ashforth et al (2008). Fein (2014) report that these authors mostly subscribe to the overall idea that the complexity of corruption can best be dealt with by using broader and more complex perspectives on the issue which is mostly understood as the challenge to integrate as many relevant aspects as necessary and/or possible. These papers suggest broader perspectives and contextual sensitivity as explicit goals of corruption research. Lange (2008) calls for epistemological complexity and theoretical integration. Shadnam and Lawrence (2011) stress that morality in organizations is embedded in *nested systems* of individuals, organizations and moral communities. Morality is neither personal nor universal but always situated in specific social and historical context. They urge for *thick* descriptions based on constructivism, i.e. for a more systematic inclusion of social and cultural contexts as well as methods and perspectives able to provide access to individual understandings of organization members' own behaviors (Fein, 2014).

Rabl (2011) conceives corrupt behavior as the result of a complex interplay of motivations, volitions, emotions and cognitions in an individual's decision-making process. von Maravic (2007) suggests combining institutional and behavioral perspectives, basing his studies on the theory of Actor-Centered Institutionalism of Scharpf (1997). Luo (2004) considers, amongst others, aspects such as organizational design, task and institutional environments, organizational behaviors and anti-corruption practices. Ashforth et al., (2008) view corruption in organizational life as a systemic and synergistic phenomenon and call for conceptual work that is integrative, interactionist and processual in nature (Fein, 2014).

Fein and Weibler (2014) conclude that these authors of the Organization Studies domains perceive corruption as a challenging complex phenomenon in the sense that they acknowledge multiple interrelations of structural/institutional/organizational with personal/motivational/behavioral aspects of corruption as well as with its social cultural and historical dimensions.

Political Science: It is seen from literature that until just a few decades ago, the historical perspectives on corruption described earlier were more or less same as those of Political Science as a discipline, viewing the phenomenon in the narrow mode and more as an individual-specific point of view. In recent times, however, as societies and polities evolved, so has the discipline of Political Science and its perspectives on corruption.

O'Hara, (2014) applies some of the core general principles of heterodox political economy — especially with an institutional and evolutionary emphasis — to the topic of corruption as a global, regional, and national phenomenon. O'Hara states that modern classical approaches have been developed, with considerable attention being given to empirical and institutional evidence and theory, as well as linking systemic corruption to matters, such as the rise of the modern state, corporate power, non-profit organizations, elite families, and other institutions. Corruption in this systemic sense is the abuse of power for private benefit against the common good based on the actions of bribery, fraud, extortion, embezzlement, state capture, nepotism and others.

CHART-A – Perspectives on Corruption (Based on Jancsics, 2014)

History	a)	Describes how corruption has historically changed as also changes in the value system defining what is legitimate and/or corrupt (Engels, Fahrmeir & Nutzenadel, 2009).
	b)	Historical relativity of corruption (Volkov, 2000)
	c)	Corruption is a typical product of modernization (Fein 2014)
Economics	a)	Agent defrauds the principal and gives illegal gain to customer/himself (Rose-Ackerman, 2000)
	b)	Emphasizes the need for appropriate incentives and punishments (Bardhan, 2006)
	c)	"Use of public office for private gain" (Grey and Kaufmann, 1998)
Law	a)	There is a close and contradictory relationship between formal legal order and corruption (Anders & Nuijten, 2007)
Political Science	a)	Perspectives similar to Economics/Historical perspectives originally.
	b)	Recently, modern classical approaches have been developed with attention to empirical & institutional evidence and theory, as well as linking systemic corruption to matters such as rise of the modern state, corporate power, non-profit organizations, elite families and other institutions (O'Hara, 2014).
Psychology	a)	Micro level analysis such as motives of bribe taking (Richter 1989), lack of integrity, empathy; self control or moral identity; low levels of cognitive mood development, diagnosable psycho-pathology, etc. (from Ashforth et al, 2008).
	b)	Suggests that corruption can be eliminated only if organizations can root out and keep out such individuals (Lanyon & Goodstein, 2004)
	c)	Delimited to outcomes at individual and sub group level (Ashforth et al, 2008)
Anthropology	a)	Micro level behavioral practices such as reciprocity as means of establishing mutual trust (Mauss, 2002)
	b)	Too strong or premature value judgments may prohibit appropriate factual analysis of behavioral logics and resulting social structure (Fein 2014).

Sociology	a)	Corruption is an action that deviates from the general Normative expectations, in search for a benefit for a person or a restricted group (Freisitzer, 1981)
	b)	'Economical' explanation could exist only in 'cold' societies (Jonnies, 1947) and the principal-agent relationship is socially conditioned (Lopez & Santos 2014)
	c)	Corruption is a phenomenon of perception (von Alemann, 2005)
Culture & Religion	a)	Very few studies where culture/religion is an explanatory variable
	b)	Cultural and religious differences are related to perceived corruption (Mensah, 2014, North et al, 2013)

Micro level Perspective
Organizational Corruption is a result of rational decisions of individual actors.

Macro Perspectives
Focus on social norms and structural arrangements that facilitate Organizational Corruption.

Relational Approaches
Examine social interactions and networks among corrupt actors.

Organizational Corruption
Furthering of individual interests by one or more organizational actors through the intentional misdirection of organizational resources, this behavior being ostensibly on behalf of the organization (Lange, 2008)

Organizational Studies such as Organizational Behavior, Behavioral Ethics, Management Studies and Behavioral Economics.	a)	The complexity of corruption can best be dealt with by using broader and more complex perspectives on the issue, integrating as many relevant aspects as possible (Fein & Weibler 2014)
	b)	Morality in organizations is embedded in nested systems of individuals, organizations and moral communities (Shadnam & Lawrence, 2011)
	c)	Corrupt behavior in the result of a complex interplay of motivation, volitions, emotions and cognitions in an individual's decision making process (Rabl, 2011)
	d)	There is much need for conceptual work that is integrative, interactionist and processual in nature (Ashforth et al, 2008)

In this chapter we have reviewed (not exhaustively) several of the perspectives on OC from the domains of History, Economics, Sociology, Psychology, Anthropology, Legal Perspective, Culture and Religion, Political Science, and Organization Studies such as Organizational Behavior, Behavioral Ethics and Management Studies. Jancsics (2014) has suggested that many studies of corruption fall into three major categories: one, a micro-level perspective where corruption is viewed as resulting from rational decisions of individual actors; two, a macro perspective that focuses on social norms and the structural arrangements that facilitate corruption; and three, a relational approach that examines social interactions and networks among corrupt actors. Drawing from Jancsics (2014) we have presented the aforesaid twelve perspectives in the form of Chart-A above.

The perspectives of History, Economics, Law, Political Science, Psychology and Anthropology are seen to fall broadly under the micro-level rational-actor perspective. The Sociology and Culture/Religion perspectives fall under the Macro (Structural) group and the Organization Studies perspectives of Organizational Studies, Behavioral Ethics and Management Studies are included under the Relational Approach based on the above discussion.

*

The main aim of this chapter was to give a broad idea about the complex and multidimensional nature of the phenomenon of organizational corruption and how different streams of research have attempted to analyze the phenomenon from their theoretical perspectives. Later as we move to study the definitions and theories behind corruption, the perspectives discussed in this chapter will help to appreciate those new learnings better, since the forthcoming theories also fall under these disciplines' perspectives.

In the next chapter, we place corruption in the context of other organizational outcomes of an unethical nature (or bordering on the unethical), literally as well as graphically. Later, we look at the theories that have attempted to explain corruption in organizations in the three groupings described above: micro, macro and relational groupings, before proceeding to look at effects of OC and measurement of corruption later in the book.

*

Chapter III

Corruption in context of Organizational Misconduct

*

Though Corruption in organization is a vast, widely discussed and analyzed topic by itself, it is but one of several established Organizational Misconducts like Organizational Misbehavior, Rude Behavior, Organizational Deviance, etc. This Chapter places Corruption is the context of all the Organizational Misconducts, developing a tabular as well as graphical representation for this analysis. We will try to see what it has in common with, and how it is different from the other forms of unethical behavior.

*

"Conduct in Organizations"

From an organizational perspective, Corruption is seen as one of the common forms of Organizational misconduct. Greve, Palmer and Pozner (2010) define organizational misconduct as 'behavior in or by an organization that a *social-control agent* judges to transgress a line separating right from wrong; where such a line can separate legal, ethical, and socially responsible behavior from their antitheses'. A social-control agent is any actor who represents a collectivity and who can impose sanctions on the organization. According to this definition, the judgment by the social control agent is very important because that is what decides the difference between the right and the wrong and by how much. The reader might recall from Chapter 2 that corruption has often been based on the perspective of the one who perceives it; and the 'social-control agent' also works on the same lines. Greve et al. (2010) consider the world polity (i.e., international governing bodies), the state (i.e., national and local governmental bodies), and professional associations (e.g., the American Medical Association, the Institute of Chartered Accountants of India) as examples of social control agents. Almost all countries have their national equivalents for such organizations. Each of these entities represents a larger collectivity, and has the capacity to impose significant sanctions on its behalf. They omit more general audiences such as customers, or specific-interest groups without an official standing such as non-governmental organizations or lobby groups from the group of social-control agents, which, some say, is an area of weakness in the justification of their efforts for the society as a whole. Notwithstanding these anomalies, all such lobbies or pressure groups are not full-fledged 'social-control' agents and even media is considered only an 'intermediate' level of social-control agents (Greve et al., 2010)

It has been pointed out that misconduct in organization can be approached from two broad perspectives – moral philosophy and deviance perspective – with six different (but with overlaps) methods of defining various types of misconduct (Lefkowitz, 2014). These six areas include Unethical Behavior (UB), Incivility or rude behavior (RB) Organizational Deviance (OD) Organizational Misbehavior (OM) Counter-productive Workplace Behavior (CWB) and Corruption (CHART B). These areas, with their alternate names and defining characteristics are discussed below so as to distinguish the other members of this group from corruption.

Unethical Behavior (UB) is frequently defined as the violation of widely accepted moral principles such as respect for persons, beneficence (an obligation to do good, when appropriate and feasible), non-malfeasance (a more universal obligation to avoid unjustifiably causing harm), fairness or justice; and interpersonal virtues such as fidelity, responsibility, integrity and fulfilling legitimate duties & obligations (Gauthier, 2008). UB's essential features are that it may involve intentional (like Corruption, CWB etc.) self-serving, breach of trust (again like Corruption) or unintentional failure to meet one's own standards (like attempting to do the right thing, but succumbing to self-serving temptations or failing to resolve a value conflict effectively) (Banaji et al, 2003). Corruption therefore, is certainly a form of unethical behavior, but holds a special position in this domain, as we see below.

Rude Behavior (RB) could also be called 'incivility' or 'nuisance behavior' (Lewis, 2004). RB is generally intended to mean behavior that fails to confirm with social expectations and so is unconventional, rude, often antisocial or hostile. But scholars have pointed out that perhaps, depending on the harm caused and the norm violated, some forms of RB can become UB (Lefkowitz, 2009). RB can be intentional or unintentional. Generally, RB causes minor harm, disrespect or insult to others.

Organizational Deviance (from Sociology domain) (OD) has been defined as an activity, event or circumstance occurring in and/or produced by a formal organization that deviates from both formal design goals and normalized standards or expectations either in the fact of its occurrence or in its consequences, and produces a sub-optimal outcome (Vaughn, 1999). We consider OD as different from 'Workplace' Deviance which is voluntary behavior that violates organizational norms, policies, and rules, with the potential of jeopardizing the well-being of the organization or its members (Robinson and Bennett 1995).WD is closely similar to CWB, described below, and hence we consider WD and CWB as one, for our purpose. In OD, there may or may not be violation of general moral principles; but generally, only organizational norms have been clearly violated. OD may also be intentional, unintentional or even accidental whereas Workplace Deviance (or CWB) is *intentional*. OD can cause harm to others or to the organization itself. Its measurement is entirely at organizational/micro/macro levels.

Organizational Misbehavior (OM) is defined as any *intentional* action by member(s) of the organization that defies and violates the shared organizational norms and expectations and/or core societal values, mores or standards of proper conduct (Vardi and Weitz, 2004). It is very similar to Corruption in its negative aspect, and somewhat overlaps with Unethical Behavior (UB) and Organizational Deviance (OD) depending on the norms violated.

OM is always strictly with intentional motivation, and the focus is on norm-violations, irrespective of the nature of the consequences. It is different from Corruption in the aspect that Corruption *necessarily* involves a breach of trust or faith, whereas OM need not. It is some-what an oxymoron that some forms of 'ethically good' behavior (e.g. whistle blowing, preventing execution of certain policies which could possibly be corrupt or against the common good) can be considered as Organizational Misbehavior.

Counterproductive Work-place Behavior (CWB) or Deviant Workplace Behavior or Workplace Deviance is generally defined as voluntary or intentional behavior that violates significant organizational norms and in so doing, threatens the well-being of an organization, its members or both (Robinson & Bennet, 1995). Counterproductive work behaviors (CWBs) are deliberate actions that harm the organization or its members (O'Boyle, Forsyth & O'Boyle, 2011).

Some authors view organizational norms as consonant with basic moral standards as well as traditional community standards (Bennet & Robinson, 2000). CWB & OM are similar in that organizational/public norms or expectations are violated. But they need not always necessarily be against moral norms. Such examples for CWB are use of office phone for a personal work, wasting time at work talking to co-workers etc.(We must however, point out that in the modern work place, particularly in organizations engaged in businesses related to Information technology or IT Enabled services these forms of socialization, building relationships etc. are encouraged to some extent for motivational purposes.). Where OM & Corruption assume that the organizational norms may or may not be consonant with moral/community standards, CWB assumes that they are, and their violation means violation of community standards and can only have harmful effects on the organization, even including violence (Kelloworng et al 2006). They include a variety of acts that can be directed toward organizations (e.g. destroying organizational property, purposely doing work incorrectly, and taking unauthorized work breaks) or toward other people (e.g. Assaulting a coworker, insulting others, shouting at someone etc.).

CHART-B: **Placing Corruption in context of Organizational Misconduct.**

Unethical Behavior: *Intentional, self-serving breach of trust or unintentional failure to meet one's own standards:* (From Banaji, et al, 2003) Violates moral principles and involves harm or wrong-doing to others (Gauthier 2008)	
Not involving Breach of Trust or Faith (Sometimes unethical, when taken to extreme level)	*Involving Breach of Trust or Faith* (Always Unethical)

Not involving Breach of Trust or Faith (Sometimes unethical, when taken to extreme level)

(a) **Incivility or rude behavior** – (Lewis 2004)
- Violating conventional social norms
- May be intentional or unintentional
- Minor harm or insult to others (Lewis 2004)
E.g. Impolite behavior to co workers.

(b) **Organizational Misbehavior** (Wardi & Weitz, 2004)
- Violation of organizational and/or public norms
- Intentional violation for self or for organization
- Substantial or minor harm (or benefit) to others or to the organization, depending on norms violated, some can even be with intentions of positive impact.
E.g. Disobedience, Whistle blowing, Obstructive behavior.

(c) **Counterproductive Workplace Behavior** or **Deviant work place behavior** or **Workplace Deviance** (Robinson & Bennet, 1995)
- Violation of organizational and public norms
- Intentional, self-serving actions
- Substantial or minor harm to others or to the organization including violence
E.g. Wasting time at work, Violence, Arson in the workplace.

Involving Breach of Trust or Faith (Always Unethical)

(a) **Corruption** Ashforth et al (2008)
- Violation of public/moral norms or trust/faith
- Intentional breach of trust
- For personal or collective gain
- Causes harm to others or to organization
E.g. Bribery, Fraud, Theft, Misappropriation.

Not normally counted as unethical behavior

(a) **Organizational Deviance** (from Sociology) Vaughn, 1999
- Violation of organizational norms but not necessarily moral/public norms (Vaughn 2004)
- May be intentional, unintentional or even accidental
- Causes harm to others or organization: sub-optimal outcomes for the organization.
- Generally not considered as unethical behavior unless it begins to involve violation of moral norms of society/organization.
E.g.: Organization badly performing due to sloth or negativity

CWB is often considered an umbrella term that subsumes, in part or whole, similar constructs concerning harmful behaviors at work, including aggression, deviance, retaliation, and revenge (Spector & Fox, 2010). According to Berry, Carpenter, and Barratt (2012) each type of CWB was treated, until recently, as a series of discrete incidents, resulting in separate literatures that focused on the measurement of specific CWBs, such as theft or harassment. Although there are conceptual distinctions between these related constructs, recent studies (e.g. Spector & Fox, 2010) consider them a broad class of behaviors (Cohen A, 2016).

Corruption: Numerous Scholars have attempted to define Corruption (in the Organizational context and otherwise), which have been discussed elsewhere in this book. It has been viewed as *'deviation from public norms and moral standards', 'loss or violation of credibility and trust', 'a symptom of something gone wrong in the management system', 'misuse of power or position, abuse of entrusted power for personal gain'* etcetera. Corruption has been studied as a problem at the individual, organizational/institutional and societal levels (Everett et al, 2006) and from multiple disciplines. Among all the six perspectives of unethical behavior Corruption is the one that clearly encompasses the possibility of even the *entire organization* as being unethical. Ashforth et al (2008) have described that Corruption implies a willful perversion of order, ideals and perhaps most important, trust – a moral deterioration, ...the illicit use of one's position or power for perceived personal or collective gain, and as the dangerous, virus like 'infection' of a group, organization or industry. Thus the *defining features* of Corruption are (i) the violation of public/moral norms, (ii) the breach of trust or faith, (iii) the willfulness of the act and (iv) the harm caused to others or the organization itself (Ashforth et al 2008), while drawing benefits for self, directly or indirectly.

Cohen (2016) studies the relationship between CWB and the *dark triad* traits- Machiavellianism, narcissism and psychopathy. The *narcissistic personality* is marked by grandiosity, a sense of entitlement and a lack of empathy (Smith & Lilienfeld, 2013). O'Boyle et al. (2012) agreed with this description, adding that extreme self-aggrandizement is the hallmark of narcissism, which includes an inflated view of self, fantasies of control, success, and admiration, and a desire to have this self-love reinforced by others. *Machiavellianism,* another construct constituting the *dark triad* concept, is associated with a disregard for the importance of morality and the use of craft and dishonesty to pursue and maintain power (Smith & Lilienfeld, 2013). The Machiavellian personality is defined by three sets of interrelated values: an avowed belief in the effectiveness of manipulative tactics in dealing with other people; a cynical view of human nature; and a moral outlook that puts expediency above principle (O'Boyle et al., 2012). *Psychopathy*, the third element, has been described as impulsivity and thrill-seeking, combined with low empathy and anxiety (Spain et al, 2014). According to Jones and Paulhus (2014), psychopathy has two key elements: a deficit in affect (i.e., callousness) and in self-control (i.e., impulsivity). Psychopathy is marked by the person's lack of concern for both - other people and social regulatory mechanisms, impulsivity and a lack of guilt or remorse when his/her actions harm others (O'Boyle et al, 2012). Cohen (2016) points out that the reason for the weak relationship found between the dark triad traits and CWBs is perhaps that studies have ignored some important mediators and moderators in this relationship and suggests that *perceptions of organizational politics and perceived accountability* are two *mediators* of the relationship between the dark triad personalities and CWBs. He also suggests four *moderators*: first, political skill, an individual level moderator, is expected to moderate the relationship between the two mediators and the dark triad. Second, three organizational moderators (organizational transparency, organizational policies, and organizational culture/climate) are expected to moderate the relationship between the two mediators and CWBs.

CHART C shows graphically the context and positioning of Corruption alongside the other five organizational outcomes suggested by Lefkowitz, (2014). While, because of the defining concept of violation of moral norms, Corruption falls entirely within the circle of unethical behavior, organizational deviance falls outside it for the same reason. Rude behavior is not considered to be of unethical nature when it is a minor transgression like incivility; but when it turns into Machiavellian cunning and selfish acts with the purpose to cause damage or loss to others, it enters into the unethical behavior domain inside the circle.

Organizational Misbehavior, when done with intent to an ethical purpose (like whistle-blowing or disobedience to a perceived corrupt or illegal order) cannot be considered to be unethical. On the other hand, when the disobedience is, say, cunningly done with a purpose to disrupt the organization working and against common good, it gravitates to the unethical. Similarly, when Counterproductive Work Behavior (Or Workplace Deviance) is of minor nature or ethics-neutral, like wasting workplace time speaking to co-workers, it cannot be considered as unethical behavior. On the other hand, when CWB manifests as violent behavior, with intent to disrupt working or cause harm to others it enters the domain of Unethical Behavior. As for Corruption, with definite willful intent, violation of moral norms, breach of trust and harm to others or the organization, Corruption is placed squarely in the middle of the circle of unethical behavior, while the others hover on the periphery, being at times unethical and at other times not necessarily so. The Organizational Deviance (as different from Workplace Deviance) circle, by and large falls outside the Unethical Circle, except when the deviance is carried to the extreme, such as when the organization, for reasons of its own, starts to perform sub-optimally or self-destructively, with intent.

CHART-C – The Context of Corruption- A graphical positioning

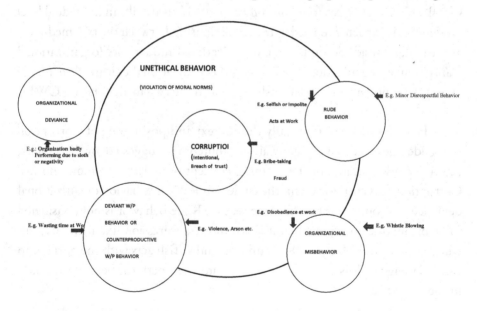

Numerous and exhaustive studies have been seen in the literature on the various outcomes discussed above as well as their sub domains and their overlaps and connections between each of these behaviors. The above discussion was an attempt to collate and present some of these varying perspectives into a coherent presentation for the first time scholars on the subject. As you read more on the subject, you will see that different authors have applied varying interpretations for these outcomes which may be also differing with the observations in this book, which are not contested here. But the purpose of this discussion was mainly to contextualize organizational corruption in the background of various organizational misconducts. We will now look at the theories which have tried to understand or/and explain Corruption.

*

Chapter IV

Antecedents of Corruption

*

This Chapter presents a holistic look at the numerous theories that have attempted to explain the phenomenon of Corruption. As we saw in the second chapter, various disciplines like Economics, Sociology, Psychology, Management Studies etc. have varying perspectives on Corruption and scholars from these and other streams of study have attempted to theorize on the phenomenon. Two broad perspectives of grouping these theories are presented here. One is to group the theories at Micro (Individual), Meso (Organizational), Macro (Societal, Institutional, National) levels; as well as simultaneously across various levels, based on the level of observation. The second grouping has six different subtypes such as Rational Choice Theories (Bad Apple Theories), Bad Barrel Theories etc., based on the domain from which it is studied. The two groups are thereafter juxtaposed against each other in a detailed table. Though not exhaustively, most of the extant theories that have attempted to define or explain Corruption have been covered in this collation.

*

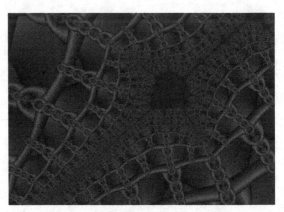

"Theories behind Corruption"

Ashforth et al., (2008) have observed that since different scholars have focused on various aspects of Corruption through their own disciplines' lenses, there has been a profusion of partially overlapping, and sometimes conflicting models, concepts and findings. There are numerous studies done at micro (individual/group), meso (organizational, groups), macro (environment, institutional) levels as well as multi-level relational approaches. Some point out that there is a pressing need for a single theory driven taxonomic scheme reflecting an overall conceptualization of corruption (Ashforth B. E., Gioia, Robinson, & Trevino, 2008). Some efforts are being made by scholars in this direction. For e.g. Pinto et al (2008) have referred to sociology and management streams for research on antecedents of Corruption and organizational behavior and business ethics for study of individual level Corruption. Some researches (e.g. Clashing Moral Values Theories, see Chart D) include multi-pronged theories involving individual, organizational, institutional and societal characteristics at micro, meso and macro levels. But we should remember that factors contributing to corruption are not same as causes of corruption (de Graaf 2007). Scholars also state that a conglomerate of social, economic, political, organizational and individual causal factors is important to explain cases of public corruption (Fignaut & Huberts, 2001).

Theories of Corruption (Individual/Organizational antecedents)

To explain social behavior it is necessary to represent the structure of the total situation and the distribution of forces in it (Lewin, 1939).To look at the antecedents of Corruption, we will rely mainly on the six set classification provided by De Graaf (2007). Simultaneously, this book also looks at other classifications and theories which are in many ways homologous or similar, and an effort has been made to form as comprehensive a classification as possible. During the study of literature it was noticed that some theories have been advanced which do not fall within the ambit of any of the six sets. They have been clubbed together under the sixth set of 'Correlation Theories'. Previous authors have agreed that just as there are many varieties of corrupt behavior, so there are multitudinous factors contributing to Corruption.... so many explanations are offered that it is difficult to classify them in any systematic manner (Caiden, 2001). Concentrating on causes of Corruption in Western countries (high income), de Graaf has used Huntington's (1989) deposition of Corruption (behavior of public officials which deviates from accepted norms in order to serve private ends), to list six sets of theories which have looked at Corruption. However this book has tried to add the perspectives of the developing economies as well as private corporate corruption for a holistic look at the phenomenon.

Public (Rational) Choice Theories are based on a line official making a bounded rational decision that leads to a more or less predetermined outcome. Drawn mainly from the Economics domain, the level of analysis of the independent variable (causes) is at individual level and that of the dependent variable (corruption) is at both micro (individual) and macro (environment) levels. These theories mostly ignore the situational aspects and the character/ background of the individuals and cannot account for the triggering causes. Their analyses start from the moment the actor makes a calculation (de Graaf, 2007). Rational choice theories have their origin in the concept of opportunism embedded in Transaction Cost Theory and subsequently, Agency Theory in Economics. The individual (usually male) is portrayed as a rationally calculating, opportunistic person, who decides to become corrupt when its expected advantages outweigh its expected disadvantages (or combination of possible penalty and the chances of getting caught).

CHART-D- Antecedents of Corruption: (Developed from Huberts 1998(a) and de Graaf 2007)	
Characteristics influencing Corruption *Individual/Group- MICRO LEVEL* ✓ Character & level of Moral development ✓ Private Circumstances ✓ Personality traits ✓ Moral disengagement ✓ Groups Types, colleagues, contacts	*Theories of Corruption* *(1)Public Choice Theories (**Rational Decision Making**)* ✓ Rational Choice Theory – Rose-Ackerman 1978 ✓ Benefit – Risk & Probability of getting caught – Klitgaard 1988 ✓ Rational Choice & Trust – Gambetta 1993 ✓ Rational Choice & Close Relationships ✓ Transactional Costs & Opportunism. Several authors. ✓ Agency Theory and Agency Problem. Several Authors. ✓ Rational Choice & Game Theory ✓ Rational Choice decision making & Institutional choice framework – Collier 2002 ✓ Decision Theories in Organizational Sciences
Organizational & Situational-MESO LEVEL • Leadership • Org. Structure • Org. Culture • Org. Climate • HR (Policy), Compensation • Ethical Code • Org. Values • Job attributes & Stresses • Industry & Organization • Compliance Practices • Perceived extent of misconduct by others • Prior Company reactions to Corruption	(2) **Bad Apple Theories** (Bad Character leads to corrupt act) • Individual Predispositions – Several theories • Low level of Moral Development – Kohlberg 1984 • Seeking higher social standing, excitement, work pleasure or cure for frustration –Nelen & Nieuwendijk, 2003 • Moral Disengagement – Bandura 1986 • 6 Individual differences of MD – Detest et al 2008 • 13 goals of crime perpetrators – Cusson 1983 • Social Control theory – Hirshi 1969 • Human Weakness- Nain 1995 • Limits of Human cognitive capacity & Information processing capacity (3) **Organizational Culture Theories** (O.Culture > Mental State > Corruption) ➤ People act according to the dynamics of the organization with one or more of the features in the organization leading them to appropriate mental states ➤ Contagion theories – Klitgaard 1988m Caiden & Dwivedi 2001 Hulten 2002 ➤ Structure & Culture theories – Trevino et al 1999 ➤ Corrupt organizations vs. Organization of Corrupt Individuals – Pinto et al 2008 ➤ Work Climate – Victor & Cullen 1988
Environment/ Institutional MACRO LEVEL • Legal • Political/Administrative • Societal/Cultural • (Norms, Values etc.) • Economy, economic institutions, (Poverty) GDP, economic equity, economic tax rate, economic efficiency and extent of natural resources etc.	(4) **Clashing Moral Values Theories** ✓ Private & Public Roles – Rose Ackerman 1999 ✓ Antagonism between two value systems – Weber 1021, Habermas 1984, Hoffling 2002 ✓ Macro Morality View – Nelson 1949 ✓ Patrimonialism in third world - Williams & Thebald 2000 ✓ Micro morality – Jackall 1988 ✓ Patronage ties, old boy networks, fraternities- Perkin 1996 (5) **Ethos of Public Administration Theories** ✓ Political and Economic Structures ✓ New Public Management (NPM) ✓ Impacts of globalization, liberalization, privatization – Doig & Wilson 1997 ✓ Influence peddling – Heywood 1997 ✓ Wrong Morality of Society – Wraith and Simkins 1963 ✓ Explanation of Corruption in underdeveloped economies – Leys 1965
Across Levels, disciplines and perspectives	(6) **Correlation Theories** – Analysis at *micro/meso/macro* levels, using surveys, cases etc. e.g. Williams 1995, Heywood 1995, Schinkel 2004, Holbrook & Meier 1993, Hubert (1995, 1996, 1998a, 1998b); Bourdieu's contextual theory of social action (1977,1990,1992,1998); various other papers from the economics lens and several others from multiple perspectives.

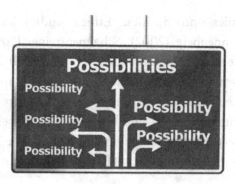

"Exercising Rational Choices"

Rose-Ackerman (1978) claimed that public officials are corrupt because they perceive that the potential benefits of corruption exceed the potential costs. Klitgaard (1988) stated that if the benefits of corruption minus the probability of getting caught, times its penalties, are greater than the benefits of not getting caught, then an individual will choose to be corrupt. The other theories have expanded the cost-benefit calculations adding various conditions that could influence these calculations, for instance public trust in institutions or ineffectiveness of institutions. Gambetta (1993) pointed out that when the State cannot be trusted to manage private property transfers, corruption might become more appealing. Trust in close relationships can also minimize the threat of discussing or to maximize the chance of getting benefits from the delivered corrupt service (de Graaf 2007). Decision Theories in organization sciences are quite similar to this, in that the choices made will be based on how clear the 'choice-action' results are, to the individual.

According to Rabl and Kuhlmann (2008), corruption at the level of an individual in an organization has the following necessary dimensions: (i) Exchange between at least two partners (Ashforth and Anand 2003), where there is a benefit and reward that occurs voluntarily and by mutual agreement (Park 2003); (ii) Violation of moral, legal or social norms; (iii) Abuse of power, authority position or knowledge; (iv) Absence of direct victims (victims are only found outside the corrupt relationship (Vontrium 2003); and (v) Secrecy in an intimate, close and hidden community in which they secretly agree on the illegal aims and advantages of their exchange relationship (Rugemer 1996).

Both Economics and Business Ethics studies have supported the observations of Bannenberg (2002), Schaupensteiner (2004), Ashforth and Anand (2003), Soleman (1998), Simon and Hagan (1999) who said, variously, that offender was male, ambitious, a social climber, and had power and decision scope in the organization. They showed strong tendencies regarding justification and rationalization and were not aware of their behavior's illegal character. They also denied personal responsibility and the immorality of their behavior as well as the resulting harm (Rabl & Kuhlmann 2008).

Many micro economic studies and experimental studies have confirmed a positive relationship between corruption and male gender. (However, our assessment is that this is possibly due to the fact that historically, women have not been in positions of power in most organizations, for a variety of reasons, which however, are not relevant in our context.). In some studies, less wealthy individuals were found to be more averse to corruption. Some studies showed that managers with an internal locus of control exhibited harsher judgments of bribery and less intention to pay a bribe. Regarding motives for corrupt action, research showed only in just a few cases, financial problems motivated corruption, but in a more powerful way, career ambition, the desire to exercise power, the excessive demands at the work place, disappointment about missed career chances or the prospect of consequence free aggrandizement motivated corrupt deeds more. Studies have also indicated that the motivation to finalize a corrupt contract rose as the risks of detection decreased and the degree of penalty and 'transaction costs' of corruption diminished (several studies). Rabl (2011) studies how situational factors – the size of the bribe, time pressure and the degree of abstractness of the business code on her Model of Corrupt action. Her findings showed no relationship between the size of the bribe or time pressure and corrupt action (though 'temptation' was higher) with higher sizes of bribe. However the study brought out the importance of concreteness in the formulation of business codes, their dissemination, training etc. in preventing corrupt activities (Rabl 2011).

At the micro level, there are some theories (e.g. Collier 2002) providing institutional choice frame-works where rational choice is combined with game theory and ideas that the *agent*'s choice is bound by both the decision-making capacities of individual agents and a surrounding structure of political, economic and cultural institutions/rules.

"When the bad apple begins the rot"

Bad Apple Theories: These trace a casual chain from bad character to corrupt acts, looking at individuals or groups for both the dependent and independent variables. The attention here is on individual predispositions and background. Greed, wrong values and avarice are cited as roots for corruption to occur and flourish. Ashforth et al (2008) have indicated that corruption has been attributed to *demographic characteristics* (Wheeler et al 1988), lack of integrity (Frost and Rafilson, 1989), *moral identity* (Aquino & Reed 2002; Reed and Aquino 2003), *self-control* (Marcus & Schuler, 2004), *empathy* (Eisenberg, 2000), *low levels of cognitive moral development* (Kohler, 1969; Trevino 1986; Trevino and Youngblood 1990; Weber & Wazieleski 2001) and diagnosable *psychopathology* (Babiak & Hare, 2006). Corruption has also been attributed to *seeking of higher social standing, excitement, work pleasure or cure for frustration* (Nelen and Nieuwendijk, 2003), *moral disengagement* (Bandura, 1986), *the thirteen goals of crime-perpetrators* (Cusson, 1983), *the six individual differences causing moral disengagement* (Detert et al 2008) *and simple human weakness* (Naim, 1995). Social control Theory (Hirschi 1969) sees the delinquent person acting relatively *free of intimate attachments, aspirations and moral beliefs* that hold most people to a life within the lane.

One type of individual/group level theories explores the corrupt acts occurring due to the generalized limits of human cognitive capability and information processing capacity. Ashforth et al (2008) point out that from this angle, corrupt activities can be explained by the failure to recognize the moral nature of situations (Butterfield, Trevino & Weaver, 2000, Jones 1991;

Reynolds, 2006; Werhane, 1999) and the routine operation of systematic cognitive biases (Banaji, Bazerman & Chugh, 2003; Messick & Bazerman, 1996; Moore et al 2006) as well as human tendencies to reframe behavior via rationalizing ideologies (Ashforth & Anand, 2003; Robinson & Kraatz, 1998) and use cognitive scripts that tend to exclude ethical dimensions (Gioia, 1992).

At a group level, studies have shown that through processes of social learning (Bandura 1986) and information processing, leaders and coworkers can influence individual antisocial and unethical behavior by modeling such behavior themselves (Ashforth & Anand, 2003, Brown et al, 2005; Robinson & O'Leary-Kelly, 1998; Weaver et al, 2005). The act of fulfilling one's role in the organization system can encourage good people to make bad ethical choices (Brief et al, 2001; Gellerman, 1986).

"When the barrel is already full of rotten apples"

Bad Barrel (Meso level) Theories: These theories include organizational situations, cultures and climates where a causal path emanating from them, leads to a mental state which leads to corrupt behavior. Some factors may be facilitating elements which can strengthen the causal chain. Here the dependent/independent variables are studied at organizational level and the context includes the organizational structure, culture, climates and to some extent situational aspects and contingencies (de Graaf, 2007)

Ashforth et al, 2008 suggest that unethical organizational climates (Victor & Cullen 1988) and Cultures (Trevino et al 1998) not only encourage but 'legitimate' corrupt behavior. Narrowly defined roles that limit the availability of information also reduce felt responsibility (Ashforth & Anand, 2003;

Ermann & Lundman, 2001). Roles often encourage a narrow focus on goal achievement (Schweitzer et al, 2004; Umphress et al, 2005) and provide incentives for unethical behavior (Ashkanasy et al, 2006; Hegarty & Sims, 1978). Roles and organizational identities can emerge that define unethical behavior not only as normal but as normative (Ashforth & Anand, 2003; Giacalone et al, 1997; Greenberg, 1998; Weaver, 2006). In short even people who are not 'bad apples' themselves can end up engaging in questionable practices as a result of being in 'bad barrels'.

Pinto et al (2008) have described how firms could be labeled as corrupt organizations (CO) or organizations of corrupt individuals (OCI). The former is a top-down phenomenon where the top management or a core group within the top management indulges in corrupt practices in an unbridled drive for profits at any cost, shouldering aside other norms and hurting the interests of other stakeholders. In the latter the corrupt activities are shown by individuals or small groups in some parts (generally, periphery or branch) of the organization for their personal benefit, at the cost of the organization and other stakeholders. When the number of these individuals increases beyond a threshold value or when the top management starts showing these tendencies, OCI turns into CO. For the organizational ambience to prove conducive to corruption, leadership often plays a pivotal role. It is a fact that senior leaders are often responsible for corrupt actions by setting unrealistic financial goals, condoning and modeling unethical behavior themselves (e.g. Ashforth and Anand, 2003; Brown et al, 2005), considering such behavior as routine or simply turning a blind eye to the means underlings use to achieve these goals (Ashforth and Anand, 2003; Brief et al 2001; Clinard 1990).

Often, failure in the checks and balances within the organization (be it public sector or private) can create a context for individuals to act corruptly. The structure and culture of the organization can be a breeding ground for unethical group (rather than merely individual) behavior, setting up unhealthy practices and extreme arrangements which end up benefiting the individuals/ groups at the cost of the organization's and/or other stakeholders' interests (de Graaf, 2007). Often the systems, procedures, and processes themselves may be outdated, weak or inadequate to provide enough transparency and fairness in their organizational practices involving external and internal stakeholders. Thus 'bad barrel' theories look less at the individual and more at the dynamics, the culture, the climate and context in which the corrupt practices occur.

Here, we can fit in another group of theories as collated by de Graaf (2007), that sees corruption as 'contagious'. These theories propose that once a country or an organizational culture is corrupt, every person who comes into contact with it also becomes corrupt; making it appear that corruption itself causes corruption (e.g. Klitgaard, 1988; Caiden and Dwivedi, 2001; Shulten, 2002). Punch (2000) points out that the metaphor of 'the slippery slope' is used in these theories. Often in some organizational cultures, not becoming corrupt like the others, means betraying the group (Jackall, 1988; Punch, 2000).

"When the official role clashes over morals
with personal obligations"

Clashing moral Values theories look at corruption on a macro, social level, making a distinction between the public role and the private obligations of the corrupt individuals (de Graaf, 2007). Organizational culture theories come in this ambit. Here the causal chain starts with certain values and norms of the society in which the organization exists, influencing the values and norms of individuals, which in turn affect their behavior, making them corrupt. The dependent and independent variables are societal and situational aspects reduced to moral conflicts of individuals. The research methods used are mostly theoretical, with some involving case studies. In many societies no clear distinction exists between one's public and private roles. Rose-Ackerman (1999) highlights the case of gift-giving, which is considered necessary and valued in the private sector but looked askance at in the public sector. Favoring or obliging the family, the tribe, the caste etc. are an expected practice in some cultures where it is considered negatively as nepotism and cronyism in some others. Often the individual feels morally and personally obliged to show loyalty and kinship to friends or relatives by becoming corrupt in their public jobs. Thus the clash or antagonism between two value systems is the crux of these theories as in Weber (1921) and Habermas (1984). Hoffling (2002) discussed micro morality (family, friends, obligations, reciprocity) and macro morality (universal values of fairness, justice, equal opportunity; duties and responsibilities, ethics etc.).

Many companies, particularly in the last couple of decades, have put in ethics infrastructure and oversight mechanisms in their organizations. But Ashforth et al. (2008) point out that what is required is a culture that embeds support throughout its formal and informal systems. Particularly important is a perceived values orientation to the formal ethics or compliance programs in the organizations as well as the employees' perception of fair treatment in the organization, the extent to which the leaders, the reward system and the ethics code all support ethical behavior while discouraging misconduct. And the perception that ethics is not merely a window dressing but actually ingrained into the daily action (Trevino et al. 1999).

In their wide view (across the system), Ashforth et al (2008) highlight the importance of trust and faith as corner stones for any business to function. Interacting with government, a religious or a non-profit organization is an act of faith. The stakeholders need to be convinced that the reporting of their services are accurately rendered, the organizations are run honestly, the oversight groups are playing straight and the stakeholders are not being deceived. Zuckerman (2006) has lamented the fact that on the one hand, businesses are resorting more and more to all kinds of unethical behavior including falsification of records and reports; and on the other hand, the society as a whole and even households and individuals are beginning to accept corruption as an unavoidable part of life, cutting across all cultures, societies and economies.

The Ethos of Public Administration theories (de Graaf, 2007): This group of literature is closely related to the organizational culture theories but varies in that the major concern is the culture within public management and society in general. The dependent and independent variables are both at organizational/ societal level. Situational aspects are mostly ignored; and no explanation is tried for why some officials become corrupt and others do not. Here the political and economic structures are studied and the approach is from the societal level and the macro factors work through the level of organizations instead of individuals. The causal path of the official's performance is from the societal pressure acting at the level of organizations. This, combined with a lack of attention to integrity issues makes the official to focus on effectiveness (get the work done, any which way), and leads to corruption (de Graaf 2007). The New Public Management (NPM) changing culture within the organizations in such a way that standards of public probity within organizations are adversely affected is an example. Here, NPM acts at the organization level and thereafter the causal chain works as in the Bad Barrel Theories.

Williams and Theobald (2000) highlight the phenomenon of patrimonial administration in many developing countries in which the private-public boundary (micro versus macro morality) concept of Weber is blurred. This has been questioned by others who say that if these patrimonial tendencies are so common across such varied cultures, it should be more a symptom rather than the disease itself (Theobald 1999). Some researchers say that corruption is a necessary phase that developing economies have to plough through to emerge into the comity of 'developed' economies (de Graaf 2007). Micro and macro morality theories on corruption also have been suggested (Jackall 1988; Bauman 1993). If Patrimonialism is pointed out to be a feature of Third World countries, 'old boy networks', alumni groups, Rotary clubs, fraternities etc. are the Western Economies' answer to the Third World (e.g. Perkin 1996).

De Graaf (2007) points out that while Scientific Administration of Taylor upheld effectiveness and efficiency as the primary goals of administration, its basic theory also holds that administrative integrity could also be achieved through administrative control. In Heywood's (1997) structural approach to political corruption, the emphasis is on the nature of state development, with administrative organization and efficiency as key variables. The developments like the NPM, deregulation, privatization (Doig and Wilson 1997) and globalization have created significant structures for influence peddling (Heywood 1997) and removed agencies that provide for public accountability.

"Multiple perspectives, levels"

Correlation (de Graaf 2007) **or Combination Theories**: These are not exactly 'theories' on the causes of corruption, but are more like a set of popular research papers with certain common characteristics. The most prominent feature of these observations is that they analyze the phenomenon of corruption at multiple levels. They contain some common features like socio-economic, politico-legal, organizational or individual factors treated across all levels – individual, organizational or societal. Many of these are 'case' analyses where the specific circumstances are studied and the causes or relationships are analyzed to form, in some cases, 'grounded' theories. These cannot be generalized a 100% but there are, however, important lessons to be learnt, at least by countries or organizations in similar situations. In these theories, the causal chain is not very well established, between the macro variables and the act of corruption, and often statistical significance is used to signify active causality without actual evidence. Hence concluding causality from correlations is to be approached extremely carefully. For instance, several papers have suggested a strong correlation between the level of income and corruption in a country. They suggest: higher the income lower the corruption level and vice-versa (e.g. Hubert 1998b). But the booming economies of the Asian giants like China and India contradict this strongly. Therefore much more research is required to determine how democracy, wealth and corruption are related.

Holbrook and Meier (1993) is an example of this kind of research where a large number of registered corruption cases were studied to arrive at the relation between corruption and several variables like historical and cultural (education, urbanization); political (voter turnout, party competition); and bureaucratic (size of public sector, gambling arrests) etc. Research by Hubert (1995, 1996, 1998a, 1998b) based on international expert panel surveys and by Transparency International (every year since 1995) also come under this category. Hubert asked the experts to say which factors are correlated with corruption and discovered as the important factors, values and norms of individual politicians and civil servants, the lack of commitment to public integrity in leaders, organizational failures and problems, the relationship between public sector and business and strength of organized crime. He found that the three biggest causes of corruption are same for higher income and lower income countries.

De Graaf (2007) cites Bourdieu's *theory of social action* (1977, 1990, 1992, and 1998) as a useful contextually based causal theory on corruption. A combination of macro and micro factors and everything in between, would be well suited as a theoretical model for corruption case studies (de Graaf 2007). According to Bourdieu, the causal chain is that a person within a certain habitus and having certain dispositions and predispositions is triggered into corruption. The independent variables are at all levels and the dependent variable is the individual. The context is the main factor which depends on the contingencies of individual cases. The most commonly used method of research is the case study. Bourdieu's theory of action provides a means of linking the otherwise isolated factors of the micro, meso and macro level. Bourdieu's theory of action establishes an incorporation of macro and micro levels: mental schemata are the embodiment of social divisions. With the concept of 'habitus', Bourdieu links the global with the local. Habitus is the mediating link between social structure (macro) and individual action (micro). Individual cases of corruption can very well be analyzed with Pierre Bourdieu's concepts of 'habitus', 'symbolic capital', 'practice' and 'disposition' (de Graaf 2007)

Some relevant Criminological theories can also be mentioned here. de Graaf (2007) says that these theories generally focus on the motive of the official; and the opportunity. The former aspect falls within the scope of 'bad apple' theories, while the latter, beyond. Of course, in order to research 'opportunity' in corruption research, models from organization science are required to describe the characteristics of an organization; and the surroundings of an organization. Criminology is a so-called 'object-science': the only thing that unites the many different criminological theories is the research object. Therefore, many different portrayals of the agent can be found in different theories. Homo economics is currently popular in criminological theories, a view of the corrupt agent also present in rational choice theories. In all six groups of literature described here, some traces of criminological theories were found and some sort of criminological variants also exist (de Graaf 2007).

Several research papers looking at the phenomenon primarily through the economics lens can be fitted into the correlation or combination theories because they involve meso and macro level perspectives while looking at macro behavior, though basically, the rational choice theories are also based on the economic man - a micro perspective. It is possible to see how property rights theory as well as transaction costs theory and the agency theory are well suited to explain business situations where inefficient economic outcomes persist, often due to the ever present shadow of opportunistic behavior (Kima and Mahoney 2005). Dong et al (2012) studied corruption from the perspective of behavioral economics and economic psychology. They examined whether corruption is contagious and whether conditional cooperation matters. They used the notion of conditional corruption for these effects and analyzed whether and to what extent, group dynamics or socialization and past experiences affect corruption. They have presented evidence using two data sets at the micro level and a large macro level international data set. The results indicate that willingness to engage in corruption is influenced by the perceived activities of peers and other individuals. Moreover the panel data set at the macro level indicated that the past level of corruption has a strong impact on the current corruption levels.

According to Klitgaard (1998) corruption may be represented by the following formula:

$$C = M + D - R$$

Where, C = Corruption, M = Monopoly, D = Discretion and R = Accountability or Responsibility.

Corruption will occur when an organization or a person has a monopoly over goods at services and is at discretion to decide who will receive it and how much that person may be given. A corrupt equilibrium is reached when politicians, civil servants and private organizations/individuals together make gains while the rest of the society makes losses (Halter et al 2009). From the above equation of Klitgaard (1998) one can appreciate that as M on the right-hand side of the equation increases (lower competition, increasing monopolistic nature of the transaction); or as D increases (the person or the post arrogating more powers on the distribution of the service or assets) the possibility of or the vulnerability to corruption increases. On the other hand if the factor R (systems ensuring fixing of responsibility/accountability, increasing transparency, systemic controls, checks and balances) increases, possibility of or vulnerability to corruption should decrease.

Corruption in the private sector, has, in contrast with the public sector, been relatively neglected, Private-Private corruption may take on a variety of formats such as the offers of gifts, bribes, the illegitimate use or trading of information for the personal benefit of an individual, company or organization and an endless array of other possibilities. It has high financial, legal, social and ethical costs, such as loss of reputation and the creation of an atmosphere which favors corruption (Hatter et al 2009). Argandona (2003) states that most corporate corruption cases involve a private party (a citizen or corporation that pays or premises to pay, money to a private party with the objective of obtaining an advantage or avoiding a disadvantage).

Bardhan, (2006) points out that in many cases of large government procurements and purchases (like major defense contracts or construction projects) or sales of assets (like broadband spectrum, mineral resources) cases of corruption usually involve politicians hand in glove with bureaucrats and outside agents/organizations working in tandem. Many economists now have models of what are called multiple equilibria of corruption (cv Bardhan 2006). Economics looks at two kinds of bureaucratic corruption: bureaucrats are bribed to do what they are (anyway) supposed to do (speed money) and, bureaucrats are bribed to do what they are not supposed to do (generally looking the other way when a violation happens) (Bardhan 2006). Another distinction that is quite important in the economics literature is the distinction between centralized corruption and decentralized corruption. In centralized corruption, some of the miscellaneous effects of multiple bribing are taken into account by the centralized bribe takers themselves, whereas in decentralized corruption everyone acts independently of other and this coordination problem lead to what economists call negative externalities (Bardhan 2006). Earlier dictatorships in North Korea and the Suharto family regime in Indonesia were examples of the former and the post-glasnost-perestroika situation in Russia and some of the developing/emerging economics are examples of the latter, with the current wave of liberalization and globalization. Economists have come up with several models of multiple equilibria in which corrupt activity depends on how much corrupt activity is taking place all around. There are models where one equilibrium can represent low corruption and another high corruption in the same country or otherwise similar countries. Here, culture also plays a role by way of coordinating expectations about others' behaviors. In Economics, corruption research has mainly concentrated on the investigation of causes and consequences on the macro-and micro-economic level Anandving and Fjeld (2001), Lambsdorff (1999), Pies et al (2005). The literature also provides some attempts to explain corrupt or corruption related behavior: the already discussed Principal-Agent theory (e.g. Rose Ackerman 1978), the Social Exchange theory (e.g. Khatri et al 2006 or Ajzens 1991) and the theory of Planned Behavior (e.g. Powpaka 2002).

Studies have also shown that economic institutions directly and indirectly influence the subsequent level of corruption in a national economy. Economic antecedents focus on macro-economic explanations for corruption (Judge et al 2011). The basic premise is that economic institutions constrain and/or provide pecuniary incentives for corruption to occur. Several studies, for example, have showed that the country's overall GDP per capita is negatively related to corruption. Some studies (e.g. Hnsted 1999, Palddans 2001, Serra 2006) suggest that a country's level of economic development may be systematically related to corruption (Judge et al 2011). Another economic factor that could influence corruption in a country is its exposure to international trade and competition. Some authors have found that the greater the exposure of an economy to international economic competition the lower the corruption (Judge et al 2011). Corruption can act as a vehicle to constrain economic malfeasance (e.g. Ades & Di Tella 1999, Sera 2008, Freisman 2000). There are several other economic antecedents for corruption that have been studied, such as economic equity, economic tax rate, economic efficiency and extent of natural resources.

Mensah, (2014) has reported several macro-level causes of Corruption: In a detailed survey of the causes of corruption, Pellegrini and Gerlagh (2008) identified the following themes from the literature: (1) institutional factors such as the role of democracy (Sung 2004), (2) the regulatory burden imposed on the economy (Chafuen and Guzman 1999), and (3) the legal origins of a country (Glaeser and Schleifer 2002; La Porta et al. 1999). Among the economic factors they identified from the literature are (i) reliance on natural resources as the source of income is theorized to be a determinant of corruption because of rent-seeking behaviors by the political elite (Leite and Weidmann 1999; La Porta et al, 1999; Robinson et al, 2006) and (ii) openness to trade and increasing supply of foreign products on domestic market as a deterrence to corruption (Acemoglu and Verdir 2000). Of the institutional factors theorized to be a deterrence to corruption, Pellegrini and Gerlagh (2008) found consistent support only for (i) role of democracy, (ii) the proportion of population professing the Protestant Christian faith and (iii) political stability over a long period of time. Among the economic factors, they found statistical significance for (i) reliance on natural resources as proxied by the percentage of fuels and minerals in the exports of the country to be positively related to high corruption levels, and (ii) general income level to be positively associated with low corruption levels. Notably absent from the literature to date is an explicit examination of the possible relationship between national culture (beyond those identified under institutional factors), professed religious beliefs (beyond the Protestant Christian faith) and the level of perceived corruption in a country (Mensah 2014).

*

In this chapter we have tried to list out and discuss as exhaustively as possible the various theories that have attempted to explain or analyze the theories behind the phenomenon of corruption. On one hand we looked at six streams of theories that developed based on the domain or discipline from whose perspective the analysis was done; and on the other we have maintained the three levels of perspective- micro, meso, and macro levels, followed by an across-levels view point. From the point of view of the organization, the multi-disciplinary, multi-level perspective is what appears to be needed to understand this complex phenomenon. We will now look at some of the less explored concepts behind corruption theory.

*

Chapter V

Precursors, Mediators and Moderators of Corruption

*

In this Chapter, we discuss some of the less researched and studied – but critical - aspects of Corruption, particularly from an analytical and preventive point of view. As in numerous other phenomena, Corruption also has certain precursors (say, 'what goes before','' warning bells', 'red flags' etc..); mediators (presence or absence of what factors makes it happen); and moderators(what controls the intensity of the phenomenon). Understanding these key concepts go a long way to actual appreciation of the final result of Corruption.

*

"Precursors are like alerts or warning bells"

Precursors: Oxforddictionaries.com describes a 'precursor' as a person or thing that comes before another of the same kind; a forerunner. A precursor is different from an antecedent (a thing or event that existed before or logically precedes another (Oxforddictionaries.com)) in that a precursor is of the same kind or similar to what follows, whereas the antecedent may be something completely different from it. Antecedents are often described by the conditions prevailing in the environment, the behavioral, socio-economic backgrounds of the actors, organizational and institutional factors and so on, based on which we have discussed various theories on corruption earlier in this book. The 'antecedent' and the 'precursor' are also different from the 'cause' (something that gives rise to- (Oxforddictionaries.com)), which is the reason for the existence or occurrence of the phenomenon. If we take the analogy of a thunderstorm, for instance, the cause of the storm would be the presence of large amounts of water vapor in the atmosphere being carried by the wind systems and facilitating ocean currents, (as part of the water-cycle in Nature), the antecedents of the storm would be the extreme hot and humid conditions giving rise to atmospheric depressions, and the precursors to the storm would be the rising winds, thunder, lightning and the falling barometer.

When we look at the phenomenon of organizational corruption, its cause – the basic reason for its existence or what gives rise to it has to be human need or human greed, from our understanding of the rational theories in economics, behavioral economics or economic psychology. Its antecedents, we have already examined in the foregoing discussion of literature. Some authors have also suggested that it is possible to identify *precursors* of corruption.

Purcell, (2014) reports that The Institute of Internal Auditors and KPMG Fraud Survey (KPMG 2008:20) used the term, 'red flags', which are 'early warning signs of possible fraud'. Krambia-Kapardis (2001:51) considered that a disadvantage of a 'red flag' was that it focused attention on cues and potentially limited an investigator from observing other conditions. Clarke (2005:77-101) expanded the notion of 'organizational indicators to include pathological behaviors by a manager or staff member, for example, manipulative, unethical, shallow and parasitic actions, staff bullying and a desire for power and control'. The KPMG Fraud Survey (KPMG 2013:30, 2008:20) noted that 21%-22% of respondents in the two surveys indicated that the warning signs of fraudulent activity (KPMG 2013:13) were ignored. We propose to call these red flags or early warning signs *Precursors* of OC.

The above incidence of abnormal behavioral patterns by a manager or staff member are examples for micro-level precursors of OC. We suggest that such abnormalities or irregularities can be found at meso levels (groups, organization level) as well as at macro levels (institution, industry, society, economy). While numerous practitioner papers are seen discussing such early warning signs or red flags at industry or sector levels (e.g. Hindmoor & Mc Connell, (2013) on the global financial crisis; Lang & Schmidt, (2015) on systemic banking crisis; Dwyer & Tan, (2014) on the 2008-09 financial crisis etc.), there are few academic papers exploring this avenue in literature. It is generally the in-house or external audit teams, the oversight or vigilance departments or the regulatory bodies which normally notice the tell-tale signs of an ongoing or likely incident of possible ethics violation in an organization or sector/ industry. We suggest that there is a need for further academic research into this emerging area of precursors to corruption which can be of considerable interest to scholars and practitioners alike.

We have discussed earlier in this book the (Lefkowitz, 2014) six areas of organizational misconduct which include Unethical Behavior (UB), Incivility or rude behavior (RB) Organizational Deviance (OD) Organizational Misbehavior (OM) Counter productive Work Behavior (CWB) and Corruption. We have presented in the Chart C that while Corruption lies wholly within the circle of Unethical Behavior, OM, CWB and RB lie on the periphery. When the dark triad traits come into play in organizational settings, these misconducts tend to get aggravated. Cohen (2016) reports that the narcissistic personality (one of the dark triad constructs) is marked by grandiosity, a sense of entitlement, and a lack of empathy (Smith & Lilienfeld, 2013). Wu and Lebreton (2011) contended that narcissists' tendencies may lead such people to engage in behaviors such as hostility, obstructionism, or overt aggression directed toward other individuals. In addition, the narcissist's increased likelihood of interpreting interactions as transgressions may also lead to retaliatory behaviors. This is an aggravation of the RB concept. Machiavellianism is associated with a disregard for the importance of morality and the use of craft and dishonesty to pursue and maintain power (Smith & Lilienfeld, 2013). According to Wu and Lebreton (2011), Machiavellians are more likely to engage in highly manipulative behaviors and, because they are impulsive, irresponsible, and lack any emotional involvement (Skinner, 1988), they do not consider the negative impact of their behaviors on others. This is aggravated CWB. Psychopathy has been described above as impulsivity and thrill-seeking, combined with low empathy and anxiety (Spain et al., 2014). Wu and Lebreton (2011) added that psychopaths gain satisfaction from harming others and they also use this behavior as a tactic to achieve their goals. They may hurt others as a means of drawing others' attention away from a particular task. Thus, by focusing another party's attention on something other than the task at hand (i.e., hostility among coworkers), psychopaths may be able to pursue their agendas better. This is an example of OM getting aggravated. Thus when the three 'peripherally unethical' misconducts CWB, OM and RB tend to extreme levels, moving into *intentional* acts involving *breach of trust, violation of moral/public norms* in addition to organizational norms (Ashforth et al, 2008) and involving *Machiavellian cunning* and psychopathic attitudes from the dark triad construct (Smith, 2013), they enter into the realm of unethical behavior, of which the most virulent example is OC.

We have also defined a precursor as a thing or occurrence that comes before another of the same kind; a forerunner. With the reasoning described above, we suggest that increasing frequency (and with intensity of the dark triad traits on display) of CWB, OM and RB in an organizational setting could be considered as precursors to OC. Once again taking the analogy of the thunderstorm, thunder, lightning, strong winds or falling pressures occurring individually need not indicate that a thunderstorm is necessarily approaching; they may be standalone occurrences with locally relevant causes for such occurrence. Yet, they may also be precursors of a serious storm around the corner. In the same manner, occurrence of CWB, OM or RB with increasing intensity by itself need not mean that acts of Corruption are afoot. However, organizations and regulatory bodies would do well to exercise due diligence in such eventualities. This is also another area where academic scrutiny is required on the relationship between the occurrences of the other misconducts of CWB/OM/RB with occurrence of OC.

"Ethics Resources in Organizations"

Mediators or Ethics Resources: Literature cites some organizational paradigms which can be considered as *Ethics Resources* to OC. Ethics Resources, somewhat like *mediator* variables specify how or why a particular effect or relationship occurs in an organizational setting. In behavior sciences, mediators describe the psychological process that occurs to create the relationship, and as such are always dynamic properties of individuals (e.g., emotions, beliefs, behaviors), organizations or institutions. Baron and Kenny (1986) suggest that mediators explain how external events take on internal psychological significance. While an individual in a societal setting responds in a particular manner to the factors stimulating unethical behavior based on his individual background, and other parameters as seen in the earlier discussions of antecedents to OC in this book, he may behave in a different manner within a formal organizational setting. This is because the formal organization has its own set of environmental parameters which exert their influence and control on individual and group behavior within organizations. These organizational paradigms have been called Ethics Resources. Beeri et al (2013) have studied the impact of adoption of an Ethics program on employees' perceptions and behavior, using a theoretical framework. They suggest three Ethics Resources in organizations that could be the origins for paradigms that could be used to assess unethical conduct in organizations: Awareness of the Ethics Code, presence and action of Ethical Leadership and Inclusion of employees in Ethical decision making. These resources lead to the four organizational outcomes of Ethical Climate, Organizational Commitment, Organizational Citizenship Behavior and Quality of Work (Beeri, Dayan, Vigoda-Gadot & Werner, 2013). On analyzing these three ERs, we can see that each of these paradigms correspond to certain manifestations within the organizational structure, systems, policies and processes which guide and influence ethical behavior. We can also understand that any breakdown or violation or shortfall/lacunae in any of these constructs would present an atmosphere conducive for unethical acts, including corruption. These three paradigms can therefore be considered core parameters to (prevention of) Organizational unethical acts including corruption. Later on in the book, we have also identified 'Accountability' and 'Deterrence' as additional ERs within the organization and these also can be considered as similar core parameters, by the above reasoning.

Ethics Codes: Establishing an ethics program begins with developing a code of ethics and ensuring that it is effectively communicated to employees and other stakeholders. The code of ethics serves as a contract of sorts between the organization and its employees and stakeholders. If it is deployed in the context of other mechanisms for creating an ethical culture such as Ethical Leadership and participation of employees in Ethical Decision Making, it may serve as a useful management tool (Beeri et al, 2013). This particular ER can be seen to be physically manifested in organizations in the form of ethics codes, codes of conduct, disciplinary rules, manuals, rulebooks of all types, delegation of powers, etc. - not merely making them available, but giving them wide publicity and making copies easily accessible in work places, on intranet or internet to employees, customers, vendors and all stakeholders.

Ethical Leadership most importantly entails modeling of ethical behavior by the organization's senior management. Beyond this, EL in large organizations, and in many small and medium-sized ones as well, is often formally invested in the hands of an appointed ethics officer (also called a compliance officer, Oversight officer, Vigilance officer etc), who is charged with implementing and enforcing the code of ethics (Beeri et al, 2013). This ER is manifested in the form of prominently displayed ethics-based or ethics-driven Vision and Mission Statements of the organization, posting Oversight Officers with adequate support systems, putting in place systems for external audit and inspections by regulatory bodies, visible compliance of regulations and the actual behavior of the top management officials in public as well as within the organization.

"Ethical Leadership & Inclusion of Employees
in Ethical Decision Making"

Inclusion of employees in Ethical Decision Making: Beeri et al (2013) point out that EDM means effectively dealing with ethical dilemmas and keeping high ethical standards while taking decisions. In the organizational context, one of the functions of EL is educating employees in the elements of EDM, including identifying dilemmas that involve ethics and values, choosing the appropriate tools to deal with these issues, and developing independent and critical ethical thinking (Dean 1992; Loescher 2006; Martin and Cullen 2006; Rampersad 2006; Stevens et al. 2005; Valentine and Johnson 2005; Yizraeli and Shilo 2000). Within the physical organization, this ER manifests in the form of systems and processes which encourage and facilitate the employees to take their business and operational choices ethically and fairly. These include systems for real time and transparent data capture such as modern IT Based systems such as Enterprise Resource Planning, workplace cameras, systems of internal audit, specialized training sessions, and other controlling monitoring systems. Beeri et al (2013) suggests that involving employees in EDM means that employees should be able to recognize the ethical aspects of problems and should be prepared to identify alternative solutions to the problem (Trevino et al.2006).

CHART-E: ETHICS RESOURCES (Based on Beeri et al., 2013; Sohail and Cavill, 2008; and Thai, 2008)

No.	Ethics Resources (ERs) From Theory	What it means in our context: Indicators (Organizational Physical Manifestations of ER within systems and processes of the organization.)
1	**Awareness of Code of Ethics** *The focal point of an ethics program* (Yizraeli and Shilo 2000). *A statement of intent regarding the ethical behavior of management and employees, and thereby articulates the core of the organization's ethics policy* (Wolf 2008)	Availability & wide publicity of ethical codes, manuals, rules, procedures, delegation of powers, policies as well as legal provisions on the organization from its environment.
2	**Ethical Leadership** *A key to the success of any ethics programs* (Korey 2008) *Ethics (leaders) officers are charged with integrating ethics into the entire operational apparatus and developing and maintaining an ethical organizational culture. Their duties include enforcing compliance with the organization's rules and fiduciary duties, helping other managers avoid inappropriate conduct, coaching employees in EDM) developing and implementing tools for measuring the success of the ethics program, and communicating the organization's ethics policy to the public* (Ethics Resource Center 2007).	Vigilance/Ethics/Oversight officers, Availability of direction, Vision, Mission statements including/based on ethics, checks and balances like *External* Audit, Preventive awareness Programs on responsibility, accountability, transparency; training, periodic ethics reviews/ethical oversight mechanisms etc.
3	**Inclusion of employees in Ethical Decision making** *Employees should be able to recognize the ethical aspects of problems, and should be prepared to identify alternative solutions to the problem* (Trevino et al. 2006) *Employees should develop the ability to critically think about solutions to problems that frequently arise at work, taking into account the spirit of the ethics code* (Yizraeli and Shilo 2000)	Availability of proper & transparent Accounting and Audit (*Internal*) Systems, modern IT based transaction recording practices, adequate and complete documentation to ensure Transparency of procedures. Control and monitoring systems etc.

4	**Responsibility for violation of procedures** or professional standards (Sohail and Cavill, 2008); (Mansouri & Rowney, 2014) *Employees should be held accountable and responsibility fixed for the business and operational decisions taken by them*	Systems for Individual Accountability fixing.
5	**Deterrence against malfeasance** (Thai, 2008); (Trevino, 1986); (Gibbs,1975); (Tittle,1980) *An organization should have procedures/ routines in place to deal with unethical activities within, such as enquiry procedures, punishments, penalties and correctional systems.*	Systems and processes to ensure prevention, control and punishment.

This, in turn, requires that employees develop the ability to critically think about solutions to problems that frequently arise at work, taking into account the spirit of the ethics code (Yizraeli and Shilo 2000).

Sohail & Cavill (2008) have suggested *accountability* as one of the measures of analyzing and countering corruption. Mansouri & Rowney (2014) discuss the growing demands for accountability from professional institutions. This comes from external groups such as the government, media, and the public and the pressure on organizations is growing based on declining funding and increasing demand for cost control, rising clients' awareness, market and political pressures. The ER of Accountability thus manifests itself in the form of systems and practices fixing responsibility on individuals for the business and operational decisions taken by them. Thai (2008) suggested a 'Legal' framework for assessing corruption in organizations; other than awareness of legal provisions against unethical behavior, *Deterrence* is a parameter suggested by Thai (2008), which we consider suitable for inclusion in the list of ERs. Earlier also several Authors have highlighted the relevance of Deterrence. Trevino (1986) has suggested that Managers' ethical behavior will be influenced by reinforcement contingencies including rewards for ethical behavior and punishments for violations. Deterrence therefore comes into focus as a decisive factor in the immediate job context. Human beings are fundamentally rational in their behavior and choose crime only when it pays (Gibbs, 1975). Individuals are less likely to commit criminal acts if the perceived certainty, severity, and celerity of sanction against the acts are greater. (Tittle, 1980). Deterrence as an ER is visible in the systems and procedures put in place to prevent, control and deal with malfeasant activity within the organizational environment, including, penalties, punishments, correctional systems etc.

The above five Ethics Resources, when they suffer through inadequacies or shortfalls/ lacunae or violation, or are absent, make the atmosphere conducive for the unethical behaviors of all kinds to emerge in the organization, the most virulent among these unethical behaviors being OC. We find that this is a comparatively less studied area and there is a need to bring focus on this aspect of organizational corruption, from the ex-ante and preventive perspective. It is possible that there are more paradigms that can be considered ERs of an organization and we recommend this as one of the themes for continued research. Another related possible paradigm, which came up in our searches and discussions is what we could tentatively call 'Unethical Resources' in organizations. These may be antithesis to the concepts of ERs and include such entrenched negative factors within the organization such as established informal practices, vested interests, coteries, etc. which weaken the ERs and promote unethical behavior. This is another possible line for continued research.

Moderators: Several moderators to the Corruption phenomenon are also suggested by literature. A moderator variable changes the strength of an effect or relationship between two variables. Moderators indicate when or under what conditions a particular effect can be expected. A moderator may increase the strength of a relationship, decrease the strength of a relationship, or change the direction of a relationship. *Transparency* is one important moderator to OC. Cohen (2016) cites the definition of Organizational Transparency as the availability of information about an organization or actor that allows external agents to monitor the internal workings or performance of that organization or actor (Grimmelikhuijsen & Welch, 2012). Ferry and Eckersley (2015) argued that transparency initiatives are indeed helping to reduce corruption because they represent an important mechanism through which citizens can access information that has not been edited or shaped by powerful political actors. Cohen (2016) points out that transparency has become a buzzword used to describe the notion of accuracy, truth and the full disclosure of relevant information (Cicala, Bush, Sherrell, & Deitz, 2014). According to Cicala et al (2014), based on the agency theory, transparency focuses on the enhanced ability of principals to monitor and potentially control agents' actions. Cicala et al. mentioned Zuboff (1988), who argued that transparency reinforces and increases managers' power and control over subordinates. They contended that, from this perspective, the focus is within the organization and examines manager–employee relations (Cohen, 2016). Cicala et al. (2014) further mentioned Turilli and Floridi's (2009, p. 105) definition that transparency is "the possibility of accessing information, intentions or behaviors". According to Turilli and Floridi (2009), transparency is a pre-ethical condition for enabling or impairing other ethical practices or principles. Transparency is also defined as the willingness to hold oneself (and one's action) open to inspection in order to receive valid feedback (Ellis, Caridi, Lipshitz & Popper, 1999). Transparency can be achieved by technical and cultural means. The former can be reached by small-scale organizational designs that let everyone see how things are done and understand each person's role in getting it done, exemplified by a lack of defensiveness (Ellis et al., 1999). The characteristics of transparency most frequently used in the relevant literature are openness, disclosure, sharing, and free flow (Horne, 2012). Harvey, Martinko, and Gardner (2006) argued that a transparent organizational context can promote authenticity because transparency reduces the likelihood of biased attributions by clarifying the causes of outcomes. Harvey et al. further contended that this may help explain ethical failings due to ambiguity and reduce transparency created by the size and complexity of many organizations, thereby increasing the potential for inauthentic behavior resulting from biased attributions. In short, transparency throughout the organizational structure is a necessary condition for reducing the potential for illicit dealings Cohen, 2016).

Organizational Policies: Cohen (2016) points out that an important perspective in the literature on formal organizations is that the behavior of individuals is a function of the external constraints placed upon them by the organization (Parilla, Hollinger, & Clark, 1988). As mentioned in Parilla et al. (1988), the use of formalized policies and rules has long been recognized as a fundamental means for obtaining control in bureaucratic organizations (Weber, 1947). In the Weberian model, written rules and policies serve as a mechanism through which members learn what is expected of them. Policies can directly affect employee behavior (Cohen, 2016). Employees are sensitive to stated company policies. A formal organizational policy about ethical behavior is a viable way for firms to influence ethical conduct (Bellizzi & Hasty, 2001).

"Moderators include Organizational Culture, Climate, Policies etc."

Organizational Culture and Organizational Climate: According to Schein (1992) organizational culture consists of a set of shared meanings, assumptions, values and norms that guide employees' behavior within an organization via explicit structures and conventions. A similar concept to organizational culture is organizational climate, which refers to a set of attributes that can be perceived about a particular organization and/or its subsystems and that may be deduced from the way that the organization and/or its subsystems deal with their members and environment (Hellriegel & Slocum, 1974). According to Denison (1996) and Schneider, Ehrhart and Macey (2013) there is a strong theoretical foundation that the two concepts should be integrated rather than assuming that culture and climate are fundamentally different and non-overlapping phenomena. Hence we will discuss these two concepts together. According to Treviño, Butterfield, and McCabe (1998), whereas ethical climate can be defined as the perceptions of managers and employees about what constitutes unethical and ethical behavior in the organization, ethical culture can be defined as the perception about the conditions that are in place in the organization for complying or not complying with what constitutes unethical and ethical behavior. The ethical tone or climate is set at the top. What top managements do, and the culture they establish and reinforce, makes a big difference in the way lower-level employees act and in the way the organization as a whole acts when ethical dilemmas are faced. Ethical standards are undermined when managers and supervisors communicate contradictory or inconsistent signals to subordinates. Behavior that is consistent with the ethical standards of the organization reinforces the message of compliance with these standards (Kaptein, 2011). According to Campbell and Göritz (2014) the corrupt organizational culture has the purpose to ensure employees' support of corruption. Therefore, corrupt organizational culture needs to address work-related values and norms of work groups, and it includes organizations' expectation of employees' corruption (Cohen, 2016).

These Moderators of OC are similar to the Organizational Ethics Outcomes (Beeri et al., 2013) of the ERs discussed above. We can see that while the ERs, when weak or inadequate or faulty; or when absent in an organization, allow unethical behaviors to emerge, the Moderators when weak or inadequate allow it to flourish, and vice versa. As mentioned earlier, the domains of Precursors, ERs and Moderators are recommended by us for continued research and scrutiny.

Chapter VI

Effects of Corruption

*

With such a ubiquitous and deleterious phenomenon like Corruption, it is inevitable that numerous aspects and levels of the economy and society are affected by it. This Chapter presents the effects Corruption has – at macro, meso and micro levels- on all areas of life.

*

"Heavy societal and economic losses of corruption"

Numerous studies confirm that high levels of corruption can have disastrous consequences on the economy and its growth. 'Failure of Nations' is often attributed to the high prevalence of organizational corruption, particularly in the governmental sector, and in the interface between the public and private sectors. As we have seen, this high incidence of, or perception of entrenched corruption may be due to a variety of reasons, historical, social, cultural, circumstantial etc. But as far as the repercussion of corruption are concerned, there is a broad consensus that it is certainly detrimental to the economy and the people, usually with long-term impacts on development, poverty-eradication, infrastructure-creation etc. As exceptions, there are certain proponents of "efficient corruption" who claim that bribery may allow firms to get things done in an economy plagued by bureaucratic hold-ups and bad, rigid laws (Leff, 1964; Huntington, 1968). A system built on bribery for allocating licenses and government contracts may lead to an outcome in which the most efficient firms will be able to afford to pay the highest bribes (Lui, 1985). However, these arguments may not give a complete picture. As Myrdal (1968) pointed out; corrupt officials may actually cause greater administrative delays to attract even more bribes. It is today generally accepted that organizational corruption certainly produces suboptimal outcomes.

The ***primary societal and economic losses*** of corruption come from propping up of inefficient firms and the allocation of talent, technology and capital away from their socially most productive uses (Murphy, Shleifer and Vishny, 1991, 1993). When profits or potential profits are taken away from firms through corruption, entrepreneurs choose not to start firms or to expand less rapidly. Entrepreneurs may also choose to shift part or all of their savings toward the informal sector or to organize production in a way that the need or demand for public services is minimized. Moreover, if entrepreneurs expect they will be forced to bargain over bribes in the future, they have incentives to adopt inefficient "fly-by-night" technologies of production with an inefficiently high degree of reversibility, which allows them to react more flexibly to future demands from corrupt officials—and more credibly threaten to shut down operations (Choi and Thum, 1998; Svensson, 2003). Corruption also affects the allocation of entrepreneurial skills. When corruption is widespread and institutionalized, some firms may devote resources to obtaining valuable licenses and preferential market access, while others focus on improving productivity

(Murphy, Shleifer and Vishny, 1991). In the extreme, it may be financially more rewarding for an entrepreneur to leave the private sector altogether and instead become a corrupt public official. Thus in the long term interests of the economy, corruption certainly has detrimental effects (Svensson, 2005)

The micro and case study evidence tend to support to the theoretical predictions laid out above, but the *macro* evidence is inconclusive. Bates (1981), for example, shows that in many sub-Saharan African countries, peasant farmers avoided corruption by taking refuge in subsistence production, with a consequent subsequent decline in productivity and living standards. Many formal sector firms, on the other hand, specialized in securing special advantages that they were unable to secure by competing in the marketplace. De Soto (1989) documents similar effects in Peru, where high start-up costs due to regulatory constraints and corruption forced entrepreneurs to establish new firms underground and on a smaller scale. Exploiting firm-level capital stock data on reported resale and replacement values, Svensson (2003) provides evidence suggesting that the amount of bribes a firm needs to pay is negatively correlated with the degree of reversibility of the capital stock—a result consistent with the "fly-by-night" hypothesis discussed above. Fisman's (2001) findings on political connectedness in Indonesia suggest that some firms do specialize in corruption and rent seeking as means of growth and Khwaja and Mian's (2004) results on borrowing and default rates of politically connected firms in Pakistan suggest that one of the reasons politicians start firms, or join existing ones, is that it enables them to capture public resources through corruption. Specialization in corruption also occurs in the public sector Wade's (1982) vivid account of corruption in one canal irrigation department describes how some irrigation engineers raise vast amounts in bribes from the distribution of water and contracts and redistribute part to superior officers and politicians. The system of corruption is institutionalized and there is even a second-hand market for posts that provide the holder an opportunity to extract bribes. Thus, politicians and senior officers are able to obtain for themselves part of the engineers' income from corruption by 'auctioning' available posts. Moreover, those specializing in corruption—and thereby able to earn many times their annual official income though bribes—will be able to outbid other contenders less able or less inclined to exploit their official powers to extract bribes. In this example, competition results in higher corruption.

Micro studies on corruption have also yielded insights about the long-run cost of corruption. Reinikka and Svensson (2005), use firm-survey data on the estimated bribe payments of Ugandan firms to study the relationship between bribery payments, taxes and firm growth over the period 1995–1997. Using industry-location averages to circumvent the potential problem of endogeneity, they find that both the rate of taxation and bribery are negatively correlated with firm growth.

There is, however, a puzzling observation that, at a macro level, there is no strong relationship between corruption and growth. *Some leading Asian countries* are obvious examples. Mauro (1995) is the first attempt to study the relationship between corruption and growth in a large cross-section of countries (Svensson, 2005). Contrary to what is sometimes claimed, Mauro does not find robust evidence of a link between corruption and growth, although a broader measure of bureaucratic efficiency is correlated with investment and growth. The puzzle may arise from econometric problems involved in estimating the effects of corruption on growth using cross-country data. For example, the difficulties of measuring corruption may include omitted variables, like the extent of market regulation and reverse causality, like whether modernization and rapid growth may increase corruption, as Huntington (1968) argued. Another plausible explanation for the mismatch between the micro and macro evidence is that corruption takes many forms and there is no reason to believe that all types of corruption are equally harmful for growth.

Several studies have shown that corruption has a direct and indirect *effect on the national economic institutions* and hence on the overall performance of a national economy. (e.g. Judge et al 2011). The predominant effects of national corruption examined in earlier studies have been economic in nature. This is particularly true for examination of the effect of corruption on economic wealth and growth (e.g. Mauro 1995, Gvetat 2006, Gyimat-Brempang 2001). There has also been empirical research suggesting a positive, negative and curvilinear relationship between corruption and economic growth (Mendez & Sepulneda 2005). There have also been studies examining the effects of corruption on economic equity (e.g. Gupta, Davoodi and Alonso-Terme 2002), economic tax rates (e.g. Picur & Riahi-Belleaovi 2006), economic efficiency (Bavi, 2003) and the degradation of natural resources (Welsch 2004).

The *costs of corruption* include less organizational and country growth, lower levels of public spending on education and health care, lower taxes collected, greater political instability and lower levels of direct foreign investments (Burke 2009). Transparency International (2006) have reported a strong correlation between corruption and poverty. Corruption affects the nature of business transaction. It rewards unproductive behavior by awarding contracts and privileges to firms in return for bribes, thus punishing efficient firms (Rodrigues et al 2005). Beeri et al (2013) point out that unethical behavior is one of the most dangerous ills of modern governance with the potential to damage public trust in government and undermine the foundations of democracy. Several studies have concluded that corruption slows down development (e.g. Gould and Amaro-Reyes (1983); Askin and Collins (1993), World Bank (1997)). In addition corruption can syphon off a nation's resources towards illicit personal gains at the expense of productive investments in areas such as health, education and infrastructure (Shleifer and Vishny (1993) and destroys citizens' trust in leadership and the legitimacy of the system (Farazmend (1999). Corruption is a key element in the inability of poor societies to take advantage of development opportunities ((Bardhan, 1997); Abed and Gupta, (2002)).

"Corruption leads to lop-sided development"

Judge et al (2011) carried out a meta-analysis of 42 empirical studies (511 correlations in all) that were published between 1995 and 2006. They examined the "antecedents" of corruption within the context of three institutional categories, economic, political/legal and socio-cultural. They found that all three groups of macro environmental factors were predictive of corruption with correlations ranging from 0.40 to 0.45. They had also examined the "effects" of corruption using the same three categories. All the three institutional categories were associated with corruption. Political-Legal "effects" were the most highly correlated with corruption. In addition, they also found that there was a stronger correlation between corruption and political/legal "effects" than the correlation between corruption and political legal "antecedents". Economic constructs on the other hand were found to be equally and strongly unrelated on the "effect" side as well as the "antecedent" side. (Judge et al., 2011)

Two-thirds of the respondents to the Touche Ross Survey (1988) among company executives in United States believed that competitive pressures in the economy represent a significant threat to American Business ethics. After almost three decades, we can still see that these pressures, and their disastrous consequences continue, not only in the USA, but across the world, from the collapse of Enron and major scams erupting in different countries. Two key competitive factors which affect ethics were mentioned by these executives. One was the ever increasing competitive pressure to concentrate on short term earnings. Another was related to the multinational business environment with its varying ethical standards from country to country (W.E.Stead et al 1990). Volatile economic conditions, resource scarcity, and pressures from stakeholders may also serve to undermine ethical behavior in organizations. Ethical decisions have several potential competitive customers. Being ethical may directly increase a firm's profitability (i.e., reducing costs by reducing employee theft) or it may directly decrease a firm's profitability (i.e. increasing cost by installing an expensive pollution control system or insuring a safe workplace.) Further, ethical actions may have a less direct, but nonetheless real effect on a firm's competitiveness. (e.g. decision to recall a defective product or to withdraw from a market for moral reasons.) (Stead et al, 1990). Mishra (2006) showed that pervasiveness of corruption contributes to its persistence in a significant way. When there are many corrupt individuals in the society, it becomes optimal to be corrupt despite the presence of anti-corruption policies and incentives. This way, corrupt behavior becomes the equilibrium behavior or the social norm. Economists have shown that endemic corruption can be viewed as an equilibrium outcome in models with multiple equilibria. It has been noted that different societies with relatively same levels of development, judicial machinery and politico-legal structures can exhibit varying degrees of "illegal (pre) occupation", like corruption, tax evasion and other regulatory non-compliance. The explanation for this observation is that different societies can get caught in different equilibria (Mishra, 2006). Mishra (2006) showed that it is possible to have a situation of low-compliance and pervasive corruption as an equilibrium outcome. If individuals expect to bear substantial cost from compliance and hope to get away cheaply by non-compliance, then the society is driven toward the equilibrium with very low levels of compliance. In such a situation, there is a general belief in the society that everybody engages in non-compliance behavior and this belief becomes self-fulfilling.

"Corruption affects the poorest of the poor the worst"

Svensson (2006) also suggests a need to study the differential effects of corruption as an important area for research. For example, some other Asian countries have been able to show fast rates of growth while being ranked high (or among most corruption nations) in the Transparency International's Corruption Perception Index. Is corruption less harmful in these countries? Or would they have grown faster if corruption had been lower? More work is required along what context and type of corruption matters more (Svensson 2006).

Effects of Corruption in State-Owned Enterprises: From early in the new millennium, ever since Enron collapsed from within because of a series of fraudulent activities, the headlines have delivered a relentless litany of accounts revealing corrupt organizational practices (Ashforth *et al*, 2008). Organizational Corruption is the pursuit of individual interests by one or more organizational actions through intentional misdirection of organizational resources or pervasion of organizational routines (Lange, 2008). Apart from being highly detrimental to the organizational interests and undesirable for any stakeholders in the organizational performance, corruption is particularly detrimental when it becomes rampant in Public Sector Organizations (PSO's) and State Owned Enterprises (SOE's). This is because, owned and operated by the Government of the country, the PSO's and SOE's manage public money and national assets, and corrupt activities lead to leakages of public funds, inefficiency of operations and erosion of organizational and National prestige and of public trust in Government. The need to eradicate corruption and improve the ethical standards of elected officials and public servants has become a major issue on the public agenda throughout the western world and in modernizing countries (Beeri *et al.*, 2013). Yet corruption is difficult to measure and corruption vulnerabilities often arise from informal practices, insufficient incentives for enforcement or adherence to standards and managerial blind spots (Fritzen, 2007).

The evolution of modern industry, the capabilities developed within industry and the efficiency with which these capabilities have been utilized, have been major forces in shaping the growth and economic strength of modern nations (Chandler, 1993). The State owned Sectors (Public Sector Organizations) account for a substantial part of employment and capital investment in many developing as well as developed nations. Therefore, understanding whether the State-owned sector performs better or worse than private enterprises is relevant in shedding light on whether national progress is being propelled forward, at least sustained at a certain level, or impeded (Majumdar, 1998).

Jalan (1991) notes that total investment in Indian Central Government owned enterprises were Rs.182,0 Billion in 1990 (Rs.34 = US$1 in 1990). These figures excluded the assets of enterprises in the banking and insurance sectors, as well as departmental undertakings like Railways, Posts and Telegraph network etc. As of 2012 there are as many as 260 Central Public Sector Enterprises in India (excluding 7 state-owned Insurance companies) of which about 50 are listed on the Indian stock exchange. The listed PSUs taken together alone accounted for nearly 19% of total market capitalization in Indian stock market; i.e. Rs.12.5 trillion[4] (Rs.61 = US$ 1 in Oct 2013).

---

4   From http://www.moneycontrol.com/news/market-outlook/analysis-why-investingpsus-isgood-idea_1002752.html?utm_source=ref_article accessed on 13 January 2016

This gives an idea about the quantum of assets managed and controlled by the Public sector companies in India and their over-whelming presence and influence in the economy. Since these State Owned Enterprises (SOEs) own, operate and utilize public funds and national assets, even after accommodating the requirement of socio-economic objectives associated with SOEs (Bhaya, 1990), it is of great interest and concern to the country and its economy, that these SOEs need to function with efficiency, profitability and control on leakages of revenue and therefore, on corruption. Today in the context of rising global concern over corruption and its myriad impacts on the economy and the people, organizations are 'increasingly turning to performance measurement systems to fulfill several functions related to organizational integrity, to hold organizations accountable for reaching publicly stated standards of fiduciary responsibility and corruption control, to identify vulnerable operational points in multi-faceted public enterprises, and to facilitate organizational learning regarding 'what works!' (Fritzen, 2007).

One of the most commonly used definitions of corruption is 'the use of public office for personal gain' (Gray& Kaufmann, 1998). Corruption is difficult to measure and corruption vulnerabilities often arise from informal practices, insufficient incentives for enforcement or adherence to standards and managerial blind spots. Enhanced information systems need to be coupled with effective and multi-directional accountability arrangements in order for performance measurement to contribute effectively to corruption control (Fritzen, 2007).

"In the last two decades Governments have started putting in place Regulatory and Oversight Mechanisms"

Regulatory Bodies: Ashforth et al., (2008) present multiple perspectives that can be brought to bear on corruption in organizational life as a systemic and synergistic phenomenon. They present a micro view, macro view, wide view, long view and deep view of organizational corruption. These views suggest that there is much need for conceptual framework that is integrative, intersectionist and processural in nature (Ashforth et al 2008)., In an attempt to address organizational corruption, regulatory agencies have targeted organizational systems and structures. The 1991 Federal Sentencing Guidelines of the US Sentencing Commission and the formal creation of the Central Vigilance Commission in India in 1997, followed by the Act of Parliament in 2003 giving it superintendence over Central Bureau of Investigation (CBI) in corruption cases, were major steps in this direction by the two largest democracies.

As a result of pressure from such regulatory bodies, organizations began developing formal systems designed to prevent unethical and illegal behavior, and controlling and monitoring systems for their business activities. These system include separate and independent senior executive oversight (like Chief Vigilance Officers(CVO) (in SOE's, India) or Ethics Officers (companies in US and other Western Countries); Codes of Conduct, Communication and Training, programs, anonymous reporting systems, Whistle Blower mechanisms, stringent audit, transparency enhancing procedures (like open tenders, use of websites for publicity etc) and clear disciplinary measures for misconduct. Such control systems especially in the financial areas became even more widespread following the Sarbanes – Oxley Act of 2002 in US (Ashforth et al 2008). Most large US organizations now have a Vice President (while Indian SOE's have CVOs and Vigilance Departments) for Ethics or Compliance Management and they are provided with infrastructure and oversight powers aimed at monitoring and controlling ethics and legal compliance (while Indian SOE's have CVOs and Vigilance Departments). Weaver, Trevino and Cochran (1999) suggest that although such formal systems can help to prevent unethical behavior, such departments or systems could also be easily decoupled from the organization's daily life. Therefore the effective implementation of the ethics program, be it a code, a practice or a measurement tool, is of paramount importance.

Ashforth et al (2008) point out that (for assessing anti-corruption preparedness or corruption vulnerability) organizations can adopt a 'check off' approach: Do we have a code of ethics and do we tell everyone about it? Check. Do we provide regular training? Check; do we have a hotline (for Whistle Blowers and Complainants)? Check; and so on. While some organizations do have such checklists, in many cases these may merely be lying in some 'circular' files, which makes the entire monitoring mechanism a mere 'window dressing'. Thus there appears to be justification for a well-implemented checklist-based self-assessment and self-regulation framework which can be applied to/by all State-owned Enterprises, which have regulatory bodies and ethical oversight officers; as well as other organizations concerned about their vulnerable areas.

Transparency International (TI), whose efforts to measure and publicize perception of corruption in over 100 countries through annual corruption surveys have captured media attention, shamed public officials and raised public consciousness (Jayawickrama, 2001; Johnson, 2004). This work has helped to highlight the variance in corruption levels across different nations, but much more research is needed to understand the development of corruption in individual national environments and how it can be addressed (Elliot 1997; Montinola & Jackman 2002; Sandholtz and Gray 2003; Xin & Rudel, 2004). As highlighted earlier, with the Public Sector organizations (mainly the SOE's) handling a major portion of the Nation's assets and running businesses and industries, it stands to reason that an index of transparency (or conversely, 'opacity') of the systems prevailing in these SOE's, if such a tool were available, could constitute a powerful tool for self analysis by these SOE's as well as a benchmark for comparing and ranking similar organizations (all owned by the State) across all sections of industry, somewhat along the lines of the Corruption Perception Index of TI for countries.

All business organizations, public or private, have certain positions in them which are expected to carry out *sensitive* functions. For the purpose of this book, we define a sensitive activity/position as one which handles the transfer of a consideration (money, materials or equivalent) with discretionary powers vested in the position and where misuse or abuse of the position could lead to (directly or otherwise) benefit for the person in the position. It goes without saying that in any organization engaged in various sensitive business activities like Procurements, Sales, Operations (Manufacture of Products/Services) and support activities like Human Resources Management, Finance, Audit etc., it is the lacunae present within the systems that provide an environment conducive for unethical behavior to flourish. If the organization is able to identify these lacunae or loopholes, in each 'sensitive' business activity, list them as exhaustively as possible, and categorize them based on sound theoretical framework, we have the beginnings of an index. Such a study of system performance based measurement of vulnerability to corruption has major implications for bureaucracies and SOE's struggling to monitor and reduce corruption in high risk settings.

*

In this chapter we have attempted to scan the effects of corruption observed by researchers at various levels in the society at national/economy, organizational, and at micro levels. It has been pointed out that corruption affects the poorest of the poor the most and this is a cost that nations certainly cannot afford to pay. We will now look at the efforts so far made across the world to assess and measure the phenomenon of corruption.

*

Chapter VII

Corruption Measurement

*

In order to control it, you need to assess and measure it. This Chapter studies the various Indexes and measurement methods available today which analyze the (perception to) corruption; and highlights the short comings and strengths of these tools. Finally we point to the need for new tools to do this critical work, from an organization-level, preventive and ex ante mode rather than a country-level, external, ex post mode as available today.

*

    Till the late 90s there were very few comparable worldwide measures of governance quality or corruption. In the late 90s, through the efforts of institutions such as the World Bank (the Governance Indicators), the World Economic Forum (the Executive Opinion Survey), Transparency International (Corruption Perception Index), Freedom House (Political and Civil Liberties and Freedom of the Press) and several other institutions, mostly at international level, have tried to introduce different types of measure of governance quality and corruption.

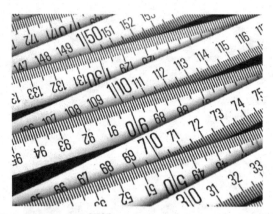

"Prominent Measures of Corruption Perception"

It is interesting to note that the international interest in the assessment of corruption levels rose synchronously with the spread of the mantra of globalization and deregulation. As nations after nations started to liberalize and deregulate their economies in the early nineties, funds from wealthy institutional investors in the western countries started to flow towards the hitherto closed or tightly regulated economies, mostly the developing ones. There suddenly arose a need not only to protect these investors' funds, but also to hold a mirror to the practices and systems for the governments and public of these newly deregulated economies for changing their own systems and routines.

The *governance indicators* used by the World Bank covers almost all the countries of the world and are based on more than 350 variables obtained from dozens of institutions worldwide. The governance indicators capture 6 key dimensions of institutional quality or governance and measure through two indicators each the political economic and institutional dimensions of governance (Kaufmann 2007). The dimensions measured by these indicators are voice and accountability, political instability and violence, government effectiveness, regulatory burden, rule of law, and control of corruption.

Judge et al (2010) had carried out a meta-analysis to analyze the antecedents and effects of national corruption. They have listed three prominent measures of corruption: Corruption Perception Index (CPI) reported annually by Transparency International (TI); Control of Corruption Index (CCI), produced annually by World Bank; and Corruption Index (CI) developed by Political Risk Services Group (PRS) using their International Country Risk Guide's (ICRG) methodology. Svensson (2005) has listed one more measure of corruption: International Crime Victim Surveys (ICVS), used by many European and African Countries. **Corruption Perception Index** (CPI) is reported annually by TI a Berlin based international non-governmental organization established in 2003 and working with University of Pessau in Germany. TI conducts cross-national studies of perceived corruption since 1995 aiming to broaden awareness of the damages caused by corruption and to encourage Government and International organization to adopt and implementation of anticorruption laws and programmes. TI also aims to mobilize private sector actors in the fight against corruption in international commercial transactions. Their index CPI ranges from 0 (totally corrupt) to 10 (absence of corruption). This annually updated index is based on surveys filled out by multiple business executives, financial journalists, and country experts for each country. Lancaster and Montiloa (1997) have demonstrated that CPI is a reliable and valid measure[5].

Control of Corruption Index (CCI) reported annually by World Bank which views good governance and anticorruption as important to its poverty alleviation mission. CCI indicators include: frequency of additional payments required to get things done, effects of corruption on general business environment, the tendency of elites to control the state etc. the indicators are assessed by international organizations, political and business risk rating agencies, international think tanks, relevant non-governmental organizations etc. The CCI ranges from minus 2.5 to plus 2.5 with a mean of 0 and standard deviation of 1. Higher or positive values indicate greater corruption control[6] (Kaufman, Kraay and Mastruzzi, 2008).

Corruption Index is published by Political Risk Services (PRS) is a private firm providing risk assessment across countries[7]. The value of the CI ranges from 0 to 6, with 0 indicating a low level of corruption and 6 representing a

5   From data available at http://www.transparency.org/service/index.html#cpi accessed 13 April 2014.
6   From http://info.worldbank.org/governance.asp accessed 13 April 2014.
7   From http://www.prsgroup.com/countrydata/countrydata.html accessed 14 April 2014

high level, Specific indicators include such things as: (1) ability of business to influence the political process, (2) awarding of business dude to patronage as opposed to merit, and (3) frequency of bribes used to transact business. The PRS group has been evaluating corruption, which is a component of political risk, since 1980. Similar to other data services, this is an aggregated perceptual measure obtained primarily from country experts typically operating within international non-governmental organizations. Additional details on these three popular measures are listed in Chart F below.

ICVS is the incidence of bribes in that year taken from the international crime victim surveys, and basically is the share of households who respond that they need to pay or/are expected to pay bribes[8]. ICVS provides a measure of common crimes to which the general public is exposed, including relatively minor offences such as petty theft as well as more serious crimes such as car thefts, sexual assaults or threats/assaults The Dutch Ministry of Justice and the British Home Office have been the driving forces behind the project over the years. A European study based on the instrument and methodology of the ICVS is the European Survey on Crime and Safety (the EU ICS). This survey was done in 2005 in 18 EU member states and financed in part by the European Union, and later in 2009-10. The EU ICS was executed by a consortium led by Gallup Europe. UNICRI was involved for organizing the surveys in the rest of the world in 2004/05.

There are a few other 'derived' indices like Heritage Foundation's Freedom from Corruption Index (FFC) etc. These Indices are derived out of one of the above four indices like CPI or CCI.

The major corruption (perception) measures prominently used all over the world today are listed in Chart F below (developed from Judge et al, 2011). The unique features of all these measures are that: one, they are all country specific indices and do not measure corruption perceptions in organizations or smaller political units like states, districts, or religious. Two, they are all measures of perceptions of individuals, either from the general public or from the stakeholder groups or experts, and not about actual statistics or incidences

---

8   From the website: http://www3.unil.ch/wpmu/icvs/ accessed 16 January 2016

of cases and crimes (except ICVS, which gives the actual data though only for incidence of bribe.). Three, they all look at phenomenon of corruption from an ex post perspective, that is, after the phenomenon has occurred or has been experienced by the population. Four, these indexes do not look at the phenomenon from the preventive or corrective point of view, but from an objective reporting point of view. Five, they all look at the economies and the organizations therein from an *external* perspective of '*how much is wrong in the system*' rather than an internal perspective of '*what is wrong, where, and how it can be corrected*'.

The analysis of the nature and purpose behind each of these Indexes shows a clear absence of- and a need for- a corruption measuring tool to look at *organizations*, which is the actual context where these phenomena occur. Further, the availability of data on perception of corruption *after* the occurrence of the phenomena is only of limited use in the *prevention* of corruption. What is needed for better control of corruption is a closer, internal, ex ante look at the organizational structure, processes and procedures (which are controllable and correctable more easily and effectively than macro level antecedents or causal factors) and their loopholes and lacunae. The continued research from this book will try to establish that the corruption vulnerability of the organization can be assessed through a systematic analysis of its structure, systems and processes, and it would be possible to develop a theory-based framework for measuring this vulnerability and use it as a theory based, yet practical preventive tool for system improvement in organizations.

*

As mentioned earlier, to control corruption, we need to study its antecedents, reasons and methods of occurrence, its effects and how it is analyzed and measured today, which is what we saw in this chapter. Now we move on to study what are the efforts being done the world over to control and prevent corruption.

*

CHART-F: Prominent Measures of Corruption

Measure	Data source(s)	Calculation	Reliability of measures	Validity of measures
Corruption Perception Index (CPI)	Transparency International draws on 13 data sources from 11 globally-dispersed institutions for this index. It ranges from 0 to 10, which values indicating high corruption	The CPI is a composite index using data compiled or published between 2007 and 2008 for the 2008 measure. Specifically, it is computed as an unweighted average of all estimates for a particular country. Currently, 180 countries are assessed, with a minimum number of sources at 3 per country.	Lambsdorff (2008) reports a reliability of .78 on average for this composite index	Wilhelm (2002) reports that the CPI explains 75% of variance of GDP/capital. Svensson (2005) reports that CPI is correlated with CCI =0.97
Control of Corruption Index (CCI)	The World Bank draws on 25 data sources from 20 globally-dispersed institutions for this index. It ranges from -2.5 to +2.5, with low values indicating high corruption	Data sources for the CCI are weighted by their source with the following weights assigned: Commercial (.65), surveys of firms (13) non-governmental organizations (.11) and public sector units (11). Overall, three measures are aggregated: (1) transparency, (2) public perceptions of corruption, and (3) nepotism or cronyism. Currently, 212 countries are assessed, with a minimum number of sources at 6 per country.	Kauffmann et al (2008) report an average standard error for this index to be 0.19	Svensson (2005) reports that CCI is correlated with CPI =0.97.
Corruption Index (CI)	The PRS group's ICRG methodology draws on an unidentified number of country experts. It ranges from 0 to 6 with high values indicating high corruption.	The CI is one of 22 country risk indicators produced annually since 1984. Monthly data are averaged to yield an annual score for each country. Currently, 140 countries are assessed.		Svensson (2005) reports that CI is correlated with CPI =0.75
International Crime Victim Surveys (ICVS).	The Dutch Ministry of Justice and the British Home Office have been the driving forces behind the project. Other European Governments and UNCRI also have been involved over the years.	The incidence of bribes in that year taken from the international crime victim surveys which basically is the share of households who respond that they need to pay or/are expected to pay bribes as seen in the surveys.		
Other 'derived' indices like Heritage Foundation's Freedom from Corruption Index (FFC)	These Indices are derived out of one of the above four indices like CPI.	FFC Index converts the raw CPI data to a scale of 0 to 100 by multiplying the CPI score by 10. For example, if a country's raw CPI data score is 5.5, its overall freedom from corruption score is 55.		

Chapter VIII
Control of Corruption

*

Just as the effects of corruption are visible across all levels of human existence and interactions, the attempts to control or prevent this phenomenon also must cover all these levels. This Chapter presents the attempts being made to control or prevent this all-pervasive phenomenon at various levels of defense against it.

*

"Control of Corruption"

Historically, many societies have endured long periods of widespread corruption. Huang (1974) examines how corruption emerged in China under the Ming dynasty in the 14th century and continued to spread during the Qing dynasty through to the 19th century. There were many attempts including large scale salary reforms to curb corruption but corruption grew unabated. Chanakya's Arthashastra (4th century BC) an ancient treatise on statecraft, speaks about various forms of concerns among the king's employees and the control measures necessary for these activities.

Similarly, Waquet (1991) discusses how corrupt practices were widespread during the 17th century in Florence despite the presence of fairly repressive anti-corruption laws during this period. Many contemporary societies are also beset with similar problems In the early 1960s, the Government of India wanted to put in place a robust and transparent system of control in the sphere of public activities. Viewing ethical conduct as a top priority, the government appointed a high powered committee to look into the whole gamut of issues. The committee, chaired by Santhanam, made a detailed study and made a number of recommendations, which paved the way for the setting up for the Central Bureau of Investigation (CBI) in India, followed by the Central Vigilance Commission (CVC) in the late nineties. But many researchers point out that *across the world*, the anti-corruption measures over the last five decades have not met with any real success and corruption has grown everywhere (Mishra 2006). Svensson (2005) pointed out that scant evidence exists on how to combat corruption. Traditional approaches to improve governance of the economy have produced rather disappointing results and experimentation and evaluation of new tools to enhance accountability should be at the forefront of research on corruption.

At macro level: The fight against corruption has become a key staple of the development and good governance discourse since the early 1990s. A majority of developed countries have announced high profile legislative and administrative efforts in this field and many developing countries are also closely following. Protests against government/public corruption continue to be an important impetus for political change and even instability in many countries (Transparency International 2004). With the continuing trend towards globalization liberalization and privatization there is intense pressure being brought to bear on national governments for practical and effective implementation of anticorruption measures often against substantial resistance and in adverse conditions (Bolongaita and Bhargava 2003, Fritzen 2006). The 2003 UN Convention against corruption (UNCAC) has prompted many countries to start looking at legislation for increasing transparency controlling of payment of bribes abroad, tackling the 'supply' side of bribes, better and stronger oversight mechanisms etc.

Such pressures do not stop at the national level and most of the large public sector agencies as well as private sector organizations are now coming into the ambit of these changes particularly for those that operate across multiple jurisdiction sectors and projects, with multiple partner organizations (sometimes with relatively weak internal controls and integrity), under conditions of complex accountability requirements and in conditions of relatively intense or constant scrutiny from the public (Fritzen 2007). Anticorruption systems in this emerging context will need to meet a spectrum of requirements such as enhancing managerial control improve system wide integrity, facilitate organizational learning and enhance accountability systems effecting changes in behavior via changed incentives and enhanced accountability (Fritzen 2007).

Bardhan (2006), looking at the problem of corruption from the economist's point of view, has given some policy suggestions to improve the state of affairs at national level. One is to introduce incentive pay structure in civil service and in general to run public administration with a smaller number of more well paid officials (This has been subsequently questioned by a number of researchers). Another suggestion by Bardhan is to introduce more competition among officers and in the market by allowing multiple officers to carry out the same function so that the customers will gravitate towards the more efficient and effective officers. Competitions can also be increased by higher exposure to foreign trade competition. Bardhan also recommends administrative reforms, suggests mechanisms like ethics committees, ombudsman, whistle blower policy, decentralization of governance etc.

Halter et al (2009) pointed out that it is necessary to improve the ethical culture of the company by introducing more transparency, communication and adherence of its code of ethics and corporate code of conduct to reduce the wastages in the company and correct corrupt attitudes. Kauffmann (2007) has stressed on the fact that transparency helps to improve governance and reduce corruption and suggest a basic check list of concrete reforms which countries may use for self-assessment. This check list includes public disclosure of assets and incomes of all public officials (even before the elections) politicians, legislators, judges and their dependents: public disclosure of political campaign contributions, public disclosure of all parliamentary boards' minutes, draft legislations and debates: effective implementation of conflict interest law separating business, politics, legislation and public service and adoption of proper laws regarding lobbying, public blacklisting of firms which have been shown to bribe in public procurement: effective implementation of freedom implementation laws, and easy access for all government information: freedom of the media including internet: fiscal and public financial transparency of central and local budgets, adoption of international standards and codes for fiscal transparency: disclosure of actual ownership structure and financial status of domestic banks, transparent web based competitive procurement: periodic implementation and publicizing of country governance anticorruption and public expenditure tracking surveys: and transparency programmes at state and city level including budget disclosure and open meetings.

"Transparency: A must for controlling Corruption"

At meso level: Rabl (2011) was able to show that in an organizational corruption situation, size of the bribe influences important components in the subjective decision making process and functions as an incentive for corrupt actors. Companies should therefore change the cost benefit evaluation of corrupt actors by setting high penalties for corrupt behavior and rewards for upright behavior which are clearly communicated in open letters to the employees public speeches company newsletters, wall posters, etc. Kubal et al (2006) and Sims (1992) have recommended that performance evaluations and associated rewards may be tied to ethical behavior. Argandona (2003) suggests that every company should have an anticorruption policy which should be part of the business strategy. Stoner (1989) suggests that a non-tolerance of corruption has to be seen as being of high priority value for the company and all its operations. A code of conduct if not available should be introduced (Argandona 2003) and if available should be thoroughly revised to take into account the latest laws, rules, procedures and vision of the company. Ethical leadership is of crucial importance: managers should serve as role models and the company's anticorruption policies should be communicated and supported from top down (e.g. Brown et al 2005). Ethics (anticorruption) committees with rotated membership of employees from different sections and levels can contribute to effective corruption prevention (Rabl 2011). Other measures that can be taken at organization level include formulation of a separate ethics code for the top management, a fraud prevention policy to cover the company and all its stakeholders, anticorruption training including case studies, role plays, business games and simulation of scenarios, whistle blower policy, etc.

Lange (2008) presents 8 types of organizational control for corruption, which can be used in varying mixes depending upon the organization and department concerned. These include bureaucratic controls, punishment, incentive alignments, legal/regulatory sanction, social sanction, vigilance control, self-controls and coercive controls. Lange suggests that for effective use of a mix of these controls, managers should first be aware that the use of any particular corruption control type entails implicit assumption about why the people engage in or avoid corrupt behavior. Also another reason for why some organization may not be able to control corruption could be that the managers may not be aware that they are influential over such outcomes as individual organizational identification and the degree to which external evaluations are salient within the organization. Misangyi et al (2008) state that the impetus for corruption in any social setting is likely to persist as long as reformers fail to address the identities and related schemers that guide substantive practices. They suggest that anticorruption reforms must be championed by institutional entrepreneurs who possess the requisite capabilities for doing the necessary institutional work to establish a new order. More importantly, these reformers must have access to the resources necessary to institute practices that will sustain the new institutional logic.

"Deterrence is key to prevention"

Anand, Ashforth, and Joshi (2005) suggest that for thwarting the use of rationalization and socialization for perpetuating corruption they should be company focused on prevention of corruption through increasing awareness among employees using performance evaluations that go beyond numbers, nurturing an ethical environment in the organization and top management serving as ethical role model. They also say that rationalization and socialization can be reversed by credible external change agents by ensure that 'denial' does not happen and quick action is taken and by the entire organization remaining aware and vigilant. Dobel (1990) suggests 7 overlapping commitments as a focus for public integrity from point of view of the public official. They include being truthfully accountable to relevant authorities and the general public, addressing the public values of the regime (i.e. by framing justification in the light of the values given by the prevalent laws procedures and public good), respecting and building institutions and procedures to achieve goals, ensuring fair and adequate participation of all relevant stakeholders, seeking competent performance in the execution of policy and programmes, working for efficiency in the operations of the government and connecting policy and programme with the self-interest of the public and the participants in such a way the basic purposes are not subverted.

After analyzing corrupt organizations (CO) against organizations of corrupt individuals (OCI), Pinto et al (2008) states that while it may seem that the organization benefits under CO and loses under OCI, in both cases the organization runs the risk of eventual extinction, if the management is either unaware of the situation or is aware but does not take action. In the CO form senior management may be unaware of the core group acting corruptly due to group level structural holds and in the violation is sufficiently serious the organization could die an immediate death as happened to Arthur Anderson and Associates and in the Enron case. In the OCI phenomenon the organization would gradually collapse by the recurring and increasing corrupt behavior of its members.

Zyglidopoulos et al (2009) proposed that corruption in an organization spreads through a process of over compensation where rationalization and action interact in a dynamic way to escalate corruption. They theorize that a rationalization that 'overshoots' the actual corrupt deed provides an impetus for more serious forms of illegality. Therefore their research would indicate that unethical behavior and corruption of any sort must be nipped in the bud and any minor violation also needs to be addressed from this context.

Rosenblatt (2012) looks at the phenomenon of organizational corruption based on the social domination theory and analyses hierarchies and power inequalities among groups and individuals. Individuals high in social dominance orientation believing that they belong to superior groups are likely to be less aware of corruption due to their feeling of entitlement and desire to maintain dominance. In subordinate groups the members also have lower awareness of corruption by showing more favoritism and acceptance towards dominant group members to enhance their sense of worth and preserve social order. Institutions themselves contribute to lower awareness of corruption by developing and enforcing structures norms and practices that promote information and ambiguity and maximize focus on dominance and promotion. Increasing this awareness is the critical need in such organizations. Rosenblatt therefore recommends that organizations may curtail corruption by developing selection procedures based on individual differences such as social dominance orientation, out-group favoritism, espousal of hierarchy - enhancing legitimizing myths, and awareness of unethical behavior. Special care should be taken while selecting and appointing individuals for ethically sensitive positions and joints. Secondly, managers can also curb corruption by influencing organizational structures. For example, an increase in the size of the power and status gap between social classes escalates the average social dominance orientation of the groups. Mishra (2002) (as quoted by Rosenblatt 2012) modeled various incentive schemes and hierarchical structures and concluded that compared to vertical structures where one supervisor monitors another, horizontal structures where supervisors compete with one another tend to induce less corruption. Other researchers, (example Bac 1996b, Kessler 2000) also support similar ideas. Rosenblatt concludes that managers may be able to control the endorsement of group based inequality and inhibit initiation and maintenance of corruption by adjusting and controlling organizational hierarchical structures.

Nieuwenboer and Kaptein (2008) studied three downward organizational spirals of divergent norms, of pressure and of opportunity and used social identity theory to explain the mechanisms of these spirals that cause growth of corruptions in organizations. They recommend that given the self-reinforcing character of organizational factors, organizations should learn to read early warning signs not only of corruption but also its changing and inter related antecedents to avoid getting caught in these downward spirals. Thus preventing corruption in the work place requires an understanding of the dynamic complexities in organizational antecedents.

Stead et al (1990) prepared an integrated model for understanding and managing ethical behavior in business organizations and observed that influencing ethical behavior is a multi-faceted problem with many traps and pitfalls. In developing a system for managing ethical behaviour a firm may have to modify its structure, selection and training procedure, reporting system, rewarding system, communication system, and internal auditing procedures. For this, the leaders who spear-head the efforts should have adequate leadership skills, a reasonable period of time in the post and support from the organization's authority structure and culture (Neilsen 1989). This calls for a complete commitment within the firm from the top to bottom. Stead et al (1980) suggests that some of the things the firm can do to manage ethical behavior are to model ethical behavior by leaders, screen potential employees, develop a meaningful code of ethics, provide ethics training, reinforce ethical behavior and create positions, units and other structural mechanisms (such as oversight, vigilance etc.) to deal with ethics. Beeri et al (2013) studied the impact of an ethics programme on employees' perceptions and behavior. Their findings emphasized the importance of the ethics programme in fostering ethical norms within the organization. The contents of the programme as well as its proper dissemination publicity and implementation as well as review and measurement are all equally important.

"Proper appraisals and punishment/rewars system
is extremely important"

Micro level: At the Micro level (for an individual within the organization) it is important for companies to undertake measures to influence the person-based determinants of corruption such as attitude, subjective norm and perceived behavioral control. Rabl (2008), (2011) and Rabl & Kuhlmann (2008) have given some recommendations for managing these aspects. Their studies showed that high perceived behavioral controls, effective control mechanisms to maximize risk for corrupt action, job design to increase transparency and likelihood of detection, clearly defined responsibilities, separated functions, a more-eyes-principle in important decisions, job rotation as well as an effective documentation and records management can exert controls on corrupt behavior. Through whistle blower policy and ethics-reinforcing performance reviews the management may find it easier to establish the employees' trust and encourage him to announce the corrupt officials to the management. The company should make it clear to the individuals that ethical values are ranked higher than the business values.

*

From the above discussion, we can see that control over corruption is an effort that needs to be taken simultaneously at national, organizational/institutional and individual levels. While families, societies and teachers have a huge role to play on the individual's mind at the micro level, the governments and the regulatory bodies have their roles cut out at the meso and macro levels.

Chapter IX
Anti-Corruption Scenario in India

*

In this Chapter we provide a snapshot of the anti-corruption domain in India including an overview of the current state of affairs, the regulatory bodies, infrastructure and systems created to prevent and counter the occurrence of Corruption in Organizations both public and private, in India. We have drawn from several public reports from the Central Vigilance Commission of India, the CVC Manual, and published reports and papers from Transparency International and World Bank in compiling this Chapter; and we are deeply indebted to these organizations for the use of their published reports.

*

"The Indian Scene"

We have seen from the discussions in the earlier chapters that in many countries the incidences of large-ticket scams appear to have increased in industries and sectors which had been recently de-regulated. This seems to have been true in the case of Asian countries also. In 1991 following a severe financial crisis (balance of payments crisis) the Narasimha Rao Government at the Centre unleashed the liberalization process in India, spear-headed by Dr. Manmohan Singh, a prominent economist earlier associated with World Bank as Finance Minister. This set the tone for the country's transition towards market economy and high growth rates of the GDP. The de-regulation of various sectors allowing foreign institutional investments in various hitherto tightly controlled areas such as Communication, Mining, Aviation, Healthcare, Insurance, Education and several other domains lead to cascading, and in some cases catastrophic, effects in the economy. With the flow of continuous investments the Indian 'Elephant' woke up from its slumbering 'Hindu' rate of growth (2-3% per annum) and steadily started to advance. Though it never decisively overtook the Chinese 'Dragon' (7-10% growth), over the last decade and a half the Indian economy is certainly inching closer, and has definitely remained one of the stable havens of growth at around 6-8% and is continuing to invite substantial foreign investment through continued liberalization and de-regulation in more areas. The new Government lead by Narendra Modi who took over as Prime Minister in 2014 continued to accelerate the reforms adding new initiatives like 'Make in India' and 'Start up India' for encouraging the internal entrepreneurship of India's own citizens and to welcome more investments from institutional investors abroad.

"Numerous public sector scams shook
the country in the last 20 years"

However, the flip side has also been revealing. It is not that there were no cases in India prior to the Liberalization - Privatization - Globalization (LPG) process initiated in the early 90's. There were occasional reports of allegations and investigations of big ticket cases earlier too (e.g. the 'Bofors' Case of 1980's). It is in the LPG era with the inflow of massive investments and the easing of restrictions of the 'License Raj' that more cases emerged particularly in the newly liberalized sectors in India, just as in many other newly deregulated economies.. If we scan the court case judgements awarding punishments in cases, newspaper reports and collated information from reliable sources pertaining to the last decade of the last millennium and the first one of this millennium, we can see that several big ticket cases have been investigated by the Indian Government and the wrong-doers brought to justice. Several of these cases involved corporate transactions and private sector players like Satyam Computer Services (2009), private trader Harshad Mehta (1991), private trader Ketan Mehta (2001) and so on. Irrespective of the sector or domain involved, all these cases reveal a combination of non-transparent procedures, violation of laid down manuals and codes and misuse of discretionary powers.

The steadily improving positioning of India on the Corruption Perception Index published by Transparency International over the past decade points to the continuous focus and corrective measures taken by successive Governments and Institutions in the country. The current Government has also been seen to be quite serious on anti-corruption efforts, initiating a slew of measures to increase transparency, do away with obsolete laws, systems and processes, as it is further liberalizing and opening up economy while simultaneously trying to keep a tight check on corruption of any sort.

Threats

The biggest threat posed by corruption is as *challenges to governance.* Despite (and also to sustain in the long term) the enviable high rate of economic growth as compared to developed economies, a huge chunk of the public money is being spent in crucial areas of Health, Employment, Education and Rural Development. These *development areas* are badly plagued through leakages in the system. A former Prime Minister of India had aptly observed about three decades ago that out of every rupee spent by the Government as subsidies only about 17 or 18 paise used to reach the ultimate beneficiary. This scenario has now been tackled through some decisive action from the Government and we are experiencing considerable improvements. These include the introduction of 'Aadhar' (Universal Identification Number for all Citizens) linking these Aadhar numbers with personal bank accounts, opening of millions of zero balance bank accounts and direct transfer of subsidies into the beneficiary bank accounts thereby obviating possibilities of misuse by middle men.

Despite the opening of the economy and simplification of rules and procedures there is a lot more to be done. *Lack of transparency* continues to be a problem making the rules and procedures cumbersome and difficult to understand for the users. Bureaucracy continues to have broad *discretionary powers* which provide opportunity for misuse and abuse. Nepotism, cronyism, bribery, cartelization in tenders and underhand dealings with businessmen, vendors and contractors continue to be problematic. Harassment and blockage of journalistic efforts at bringing out corruption exists side by side with allegation of 'paid news' on the media. Use of money power, muscle power and freebies to voters during elections continues to be a huge problem in the bustling democracy.

Some people say that the Central Government has arrogated *excessive powers* with itself leaving the State Government with inadequate powers to function and solve their local problems. This is open to debate, however.

"Several Challenges and Problem Areas"

Problem Areas

Though corruption touches every aspect of public life the citizens get most distressed when corruption happens in these key domains.

a) *Public Procurements* - Public Procurements has been defined by World Bank, CVC of India, etc. to include all kinds of purchases, sales, hiring, contracting, recruiting, leasing, renting, etc. for all kinds of products, services, assets and natural resources. Public Procurements refers not only to procurements or sales by public sector organizations, but by *any* organization, from the open market so as to ensure competition and best prices as decided by market forces. Government procurement uses money from the public exchequer and loss of revenue or failure to ensure financial prudence by the concerned officials invariably results in a national loss. Public procurements by private organizations uses investors' money and is equally 'sensitive' in context and purpose. It is generally accepted that public procurements in any country are plagued by several kinds of abuse such as collusion between buyers and sellers, cartelization, misuse of discretionary powers, cronyism, nepotism and all kinds of non-transparent practices for private gain. Both public and private sector organizations are equally vulnerable, whether they are located under the Central Government control or under State Government control.

b) *Licences and Public Utility Services* – One of the core aims behind the LPG changes was the easing up of the cumbersome and prohibitive procedures for entrepreneurs and businesses in getting licences and approvals for their commercial activities, getting access to land, power, water and other utilities and services. The era prior to the LPG reforms often involved propitiating the 'gate keepers' for getting these permissions and licenses. The prime purpose behind the abolishing of the 'licence raj' by simplifying procedures, relaxing control and doing away with obsolete laws and rules is to get rid of these free 'gate keepers'. This enhancement of easy of doing business continues to be a major area of focus for the current Governments both at the Centre and at the State.

c) *Tax and Customs* – As in many other departments cumbersome rules and procedures at various entry points into the economy starting with sea ports and air ports, continue to be serious area of concern. These crucial departments of Income Tax, Customs, Central Excise, Sales Tax, etc. have their job cut out, in that on one hand they have to prevent loss of revenues to the country through strict vigilance and monitoring and on the other they have to provide a conducive atmosphere for business to flourish. Misuse of discretionary powers and variably interpreting the rules, etc. are the areas of concern in these departments.

d) *Police Forces* – As is the common refrain in most countries, the law and order forces are suggested by many as urgently requiring reforms at all levels and for increasing levels of professionalism. Law and Order is a State subject under the States' jurisdiction as per the Indian Constitution. It is seen that different States perform differently on different parameters. But it is generally accepted that this is one area where maximum of grass root level attention is required. Both the Central Government and various State Governments have multilevel agendas for addressing this issue.

e) *Welfare and Development Programmes* - As mentioned earlier a huge chunk of the Governmental expenditure goes into the welfare and development subsidies and programmes which have been historically major areas of leakages as realized by successive Governments. Recent efforts using Aadhaar, bank accounts and direct transfer facility is expected to reverse or control this trend.

f) *Judicial Corruption* – Independence of the Judiciary in India is one of the founding principles of the Constitution of the country. Indian judiciary has always had an image and perception of neutrality and impartiality and as the final refuge for a citizen seeking legal remedy. However, recent reviews of the judiciary system by the Supreme Court of India report that the judicial process often faces difficulties of being slow and complicated often due to under-staffing. The higher courts have pointed out that there are backlogs of cases on these accounts. Indian judiciary has been consistently ranked between positions 20 and 30 out of about 140 countries in the Global Competitive Reports of the past few years. This shows that the Indian judiciary does have a fairly high position from a global perspective of ethics and performance and continues to improve itself. But the system has a long way to go and, as confirmed by the Supreme Court Judges themselves on numerous occasions, judicial reforms are the need of the hour.

Anticorruption Initiatives in India

"Several Initiatives from the Government"

In the early 1960s after about one and half decades of democratically elected Government, the Indian parliament decided to put in place some permanent mechanisms for dealing with ethical issues in public life.. The Government of India then set up a Committee under the initiative of Mr Lal Bahadur Shastri, the then Minister of Home Affairs, under the Chairmanship of Mr. Santhanam, Member of Parliament. The brief of the Committee was to review the existing instruments and systems with a view to prevent unethical conduct in Central Government Services and to suggest steps for effective anticorruption measures. The Santhanam Committee identified four major areas of concern in their report in 1963: Administrative delays, too many regulatory functions with the Government, Scope for personal discretion in the exercise of powers vested in different categories of Government service, and cumbersome procedures in dealing with various day-to-day matters of citizens.

The recommendations of the Santhanam Committee were considered and the Central Vigilance Commission (CVC) was set up by the Government of India on 11 February 1964. Subsequently the Supreme Court of India while adjudicating the "Jain Hawala Case" gave directions in 1977 that statutory status must be conferred upon the CVC. Accordingly the CVC Act 2003 was passed by the Parliament of India and the CVC came into existence as a

Statutory Body. This was one of the first Anti- Corruption Initiatives in the new democracy, post-Independence.

Legal Provisions

1) **The Santhanam Committee, up to the CVC Act of 2003:** As discussed above, the recommendations of the Santhanam Committee were considered and the Central Vigilance Commission (CVC) was set up by the Government of India on 11 February 1964. Subsequently the Supreme Court of India while adjudicating the "Jain Hawala Case" gave directions in 1977 that Statutory status must be conferred upon the CVC. Accordingly the CVC Act 2003 was passed by the Parliament of India and the CVC came into existence as a Statutory Body.

2) **The Prevention of Corruption Act 1988**: The PC Act is one of the basic authorities used by the Central Anticorruption Organizations like CVC and CBI as well as the State Police Agencies carryout their functions.

3) **The Prevention of Money Laundering Act**: This Act came into existence in 2002 in an effort to tackle the growing problem of black-money. This was amended to give it more teeth in 2005.

4) **The Public Interest Disclosure and Protection of Informers Resolution (PIDPI) 2004**: This is the Indian equivalent of Whistle Blowers protection provisions in western countries. The PIDPI resolution of 2004 designate the CVC as agency to receive and act on complaints or disclosure on any corruption or misuse of Office, received from Whistle Blower. Subsequently this was further improved upon renamed the Whistle Blowers Protection Bill 2007 and has been enacted as Whistle Blowers Protection Act 2007.

4) **The Right to Information Act 2005**: This provides for setting up of a practical regime for citizens to secure access to information under the control of public authority to promote transparency and accountability in the working of every public authority under the Central and State Governments. If provides for setting up of the Central Information Commission and the State Information Commissions for looking into related matters.

5) *Lokpal and Lok Ayukta:* The discussions on the constitution of Lokpal and Lok Ayukta to look into corruption in administration and public life had started in 1966 as one of the suggestions in the Santhanam Committee Report discussed above. After several efforts the Lokpal Bill received assent from the President of India and came into force from 16 January 2014. The Lokpal and Lok Ayukta Act 2013 is an Act which seeks to provide for the institution of Lokpal to enquire into allegations of corruption against certain public functionaries including Ministers and Members of Parliament.

Some of the other legislations on anvil include the Lok Ayukta Bill, which are to be passed by all the States for the setting up of the State level offices, Right of Citizens for Time Bound Delivery of Goods and Services and Redressal of their Grievances Bill, 2011; Judicial Standards and Accountability Bill 2010; Prevention of Corruption (Amendment) Bill 2013; The Prevention of Bribery of Foreign Public Officials Bill; and The Public Procurement Bill. The Website of Central Vigilance Commission (www.cvc.nic.in) displays a "National Anticorruption Strategy" summary drawn up by CVC as the pivotal anticorruption agency of the country to provide a set of guidelines for various agencies to proceed in this direction. This paper provides for strategy to deal with petty corruption, to tackle grand corruption (demand side as well as supply side), to address political corruption, administrative corruption, discourage private sector participation and corruption and for encouraging citizens to resist corruption[9]. This paper also suggests the supporting frame work including legal and regulatory frame work (strengthening of PC Act 1988, strengthening of Benami Transaction (Prohibition) Act 1988, Amending the Income Tax Act 1961 and Empowering Civil Society by strengthening provisions like Whistle Blowing and False Claim through enactment), and institutional frame work including Judiciary, Regulatory Bodies, CVC, CBI, State Anticorruption Agencies and the Media. This paper also provides for social action against corruption through educational and awareness campaign ensuring international co-operation, etc.

---

9   http://cvc.nic.in/NACSSummary.pdf - accessed on 09.05.16

Institutional Framework

1) *Judiciary*

"The Supreme Court of India is the final Court of Justice"

As mentioned earlier all the end-result of the investigations carried out by the anticorruption agencies finally reach the various courts which are considerably hampered by huge backlog of cases due to non-establishment of special courts to deal with PC Act cases, shortages and delays in appointment of special judges and various other resource constraints. CVC has called for a National Judicial Council tasked with investigating cases of corruption within the judiciary carefully structured so as to balance the twin goals of increasing judicial responsibilities and protecting the independence of the judiciary.

2) *Regulatory Bodies*

Government has set up Regulatory Bodies to oversee working of various sectors, examples being Reserve Bank of India for Financial System and Monetary Policies, Food Safety and Standards Authority of India for Food Safety, SEBI (Securities and Exchange Board of India for Security Market, TRAI (Telecom Regulatory Authority of India) for the Telecom Sector and such other bodies for various key domains. The main concern here are that objectivity and transparency should be maintained in recruitment and appointment of officials to these bodies, appropriate whistle blowing and complaint handling mechanism should be put in place in these bodies and these bodies must carry out adequate self-regulation such sealing on fees, rotation of auditors, etc.

3) *CVC (Central Vigilance Commission)*

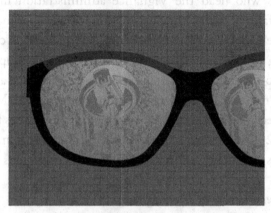

"CVC is the Premier Ethics Oversight Body in India"

As mentioned earlier the CVC has powers to enquire or cause enquiries to be conducted into offences alleged to have been committed under the PC Act 1988 by certain categories of public servants of the Central Government, Corporations, established under any Central Act, Government Companies, Societies and Local Authorities owned and controlled by Central Government. The CVC Act also empowers the Commission to exercise superintendence over the functioning of the Central Bureau of Investigation insofar as it relates to the investigation of offences alleged to have been committed under the PC Act 1988 and to give direction to the CBI for discharging certain related responsibilities. CVC also exercise superintendence over the Vigilance administration of various Ministries, Departments, Public Sector Enterprises, Public Sector Banks and autonomous organizations under the Central Government. CVC also has key roles to play under the Lokpal and Lok Ayukta Act 2013 which had amended some of the provisions of CVC Act 2003.

CVC controls the functioning of the Chief Vigilance Officers (CVOs) who are senior level ethical oversight officers working in Government Departments and Central Public Sector Enterprises and Banks. CVC examines the investigation reports furnished by the CVO or the CBI and advises initiation of criminal or regular departmental action for major or minor penalty against the concerned public servant or where no action is warranted CVC may advise closure of the case against the public servant depending on the facts of the case.

The CVOs who head the Vigilance administration in departments/ organizations falling under the jurisdiction of the Commission provide assistance to the Chief Executive Officer of the Organization concerned in all matters relating to Vigilance administration by providing appropriate advice and expertise to them. CVOs are supposed to do Vigilance audit or various structures and routines in the Organization and assist the Management in establishing effective internal control, systems and procedures for minimizing failures. As of 2014 there are 199 posts of full-time CVOs and 483 posts of part-time CVOs in various Central Government Organizations in the Country.

4) *CBI (Central Bureau of Investigation)*

"CBI is the Premier Investigating Agency in India"

Set up by the Delhi Special Police Establishment Act 1946 and subsequent amendments to it, the CBI is the premier national body for investigating allegations of corruption among public officials in Central Government and its Organizations as well as private individuals, as part of its brief. When specifically requested by a State Government, or the Courts, the CBI can also investigate corruption cases alleged to have occurred in State Government Organizations. One of the recommendations of the CVC is to enact a new

CBI Act along the lines suggested recently by the Parliamentary Standing Committee on Personnel, Public Grievance, Law and Justice.

Some of the other agencies whose work may cover corruption incidents as part of their respective work areas in the Central Government include the Enforcement Directorate under the Ministry of Finance (Financial Crimes), Research and Analysis Wing (National Security) and National Investigation Agency (Terrorism and related matters), etc.

5) *State Anticorruption Agencies:*

Over and above the State Police Departments, Crime Branch Departments, Vigilance and Anti-corruption Bureaux, Criminal Investigation Departments, etc. in the State, there appears to be a need for setting up specialist multi-disciplinary bodies for investigation and prosecution of corruption related cases at the State level.

6) *Comptroller and Auditor General of India (CAG)*

"CAG of India is the Auditor to the accounts of the Government"

Based on Article 149 of Constitution of India CAG is empowered to audit the accounts of all Offices and Organizations of the Central and State Government and submit the report to the Parliament highlighting failures and giving recommendations for improvement.

7) *Central Information Commission (CIC)*

"Central Information Commission and the
powerful Right to Information Act"

Set up in pursuance of the Right to Information Act 2005 the CIC and its
State counter-parts oversee the implementation of this Act and has proved to
be one of the most powerful grass-roots level tools against lack of transparency
and corruption in public institutions.

*

*In this chapter we have not attempted to describe the details of the legal
provisions and institutional and organizational anticorruption frameworks in
the country. Most of these details are available on the websites of the respective
organizations under the Governments of India and of the States. What we have
attempted is a collated overview for the young scholars to get a broad understanding
of this domain in India. Readers who are interested in collecting more details are
requested to access further information, reports and activities from the websites of
these organizations.*

*

Chapter X

Suggestions for Further Research and Conclusion

*

Here, while concluding the discussions we suggest streams and directions of further study and research for both scholars and practitioners.

*

Suggestions for Continued Research

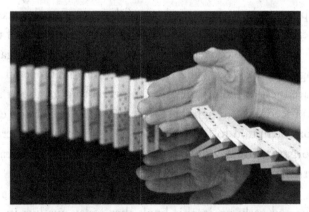

"Need to prevent Corruption *before* it can happen"

1) Most importantly, as we pointed out at the beginning of this study, we live in a society of organizations, and the modern business (and other) organizations are running practically every conceivable activity and enterprise. Acts of an unethical nature performed in or by organizations have serious effects on the society and the future of the world as we know it, at a much more significant level than those by individuals in non-organizational settings. Governments and regulatory bodies can only bring in a modicum of *external* controls on unethical behaviours in and by organizations. There is a need to look inside the organizations themselves, if they are to fight the menace from within. Therefore, there is a pressure for both Scholars and Practitioners to study and suggest means to formulate *preventive and predictive* tools against corruption based on the organization's own processes and systems. There is also the requirement for scrutiny into corruption at the organization level, that too from a preventive, ex ante perspective. After a corrupt act and its repercussions have been exposed and '*post-mortem*'ed, it is common enough to analyze what went wrong and how the world perceives it. It is however, much more important to analyze the systems and processes of the organization *beforehand* and predict the areas that are vulnerable within the organization so that timely preventive action can be taken. Therein lies the significance of this initial analysis of the phenomenon and the need to push this further.

We have suggested the term 'Corruptance' to mean the perceived and assessed vulnerability of the systems and procedures of the organization to the risk of corruption; or lack of preparedness of the systems and procedures to the threat of internal corrupt activity. As continuation of this line of research, we will go on to propose the concept of a Corruptance Index for organizations to indicate an aggregate assessed value of the structural and procedural lacunae or lack of preparedness of the organization in preventing misuse or abuse of the systems and procedures through these lacunae, which provide an environment conducive for corruption to flourish. We recommend further scrutiny of the concept of organizational vulnerability to corruption as a stream of study perhaps as crucial today as the individual level perspectives.

Having stated early on in this book that today, we live in a society of organizations, there is a clear absence and a pressing need of instruments for monitoring and if possible, assessing organizations for their corruption-vulnerability or their anti-corruption preparedness. This is a challenge for academia as well as practitioners, whereby they may look at possible theory based, yet practically viable frameworks or models for measuring or comparing organizations from this perspective. The continuing work beyond this present book hopes to present some solutions in this area.

2) In much of the literature we studied, the streams of *Ethics* and *Corruption* have been looked at separately, though it is obvious that corruption, particularly in the organizational context, is one of the more 'virulent' (from Ashforth et al, 2008) forms of unethical behavior. Through this book we have attempted to start building a bridge between the two, suggesting the linking between the Ethics Resources of organizations with actual corruption case data, and then possibly go on to make a scholar-practitioner tool out of this now-clearly established relationship. We suggest that these thoughts may be further looked at by Researchers in both domains, since we feel there is a need to study them together.

3) It has been pointed out that the current management literature is *atomized* in that existing models of negative organizational behaviors focus mainly on static individual traits and behaviors and the individual, interpersonal, and group level factors that influence them. (Ashforth et al, 2008). The resulting views are relatively narrow leading to a relative neglect of the role of processes and systems (Brass, Butterfield & Skaggs 1998). A systemic view is obviously important because corruption appears to thrive in particular organization, industry, and national environments (Ashforth et al, 2008). Our work has attempted to make a systemic and processual view of the phenomenon at the organization level and more such studies are very much the need of the hour.

4) While analyzing the Culture perspectives on corruption we saw that notably absent from the literature to date is an explicit examination of the possible relationship between national culture (beyond those identified under institutional factors), professed religious beliefs (beyond the Protestant Christian faith), and the level of perceived corruption in a country (Mensah 2014). Some of the few efforts in this direction seen in literature have been mentioned in our discussions, but there is clearly a need for more in depth studies in this area in different cultural contexts.

5) We have initiated a discussion in this book for closer looks at Mediators or Ethics Resources, Moderators and Precursors to OC. These three phenomena are also comparatively less scrutinized and theorized upon. We have suggested Counterproductive Workplace Behavior, Organizational Misbehavior and Rude Behavior as Precursors to Organizational Corruption. At the same time, occurrence of CWB, OM or RB with increasing intensity by itself need not mean that acts of Corruption are definitely afoot. However, organizations and regulatory bodies would do well to exercise due diligence in such eventualities. This is also another area where academic scrutiny is required on the relationship between the occurrences of the other misconducts of CWB/OM/RB with occurrence of OC. Regarding precursors being 'red flag' alerts, it is generally the in-house or external audit teams, the oversight or vigilance departments or the regulatory bodies which normally notice the tell-tale signs of an on-going or coming incident of possible ethics violation in an organization or sector/industry. We suggest that there is a need for further academic research into this emerging area of precursors to corruption which can be of considerable interest to scholars and practitioners alike. Another related possible paradigm, which came up in our searches and discussions is what we could tentatively call 'Unethical Resources' in organizations. These may be antithesis to the concepts of ERs and include such entrenched negative factors within the organization such as established informal practices, vested interests, coteries, etc. which weaken the ERs and promote unethical behavior. This is another possible line for continued research.

6) As pointed out by Svensson (2006) there is a need to study the differential effects of corruption as an important area for research. For example, China and India have both been able to show fast rates of growth while being ranked high (or among the more corrupt nations) in the Transparency International's Corruption Perception Index. Is corruption less harmful in these countries? Or would they have grown faster if corruption had been lower? More work is required along what context and type of corruption matters more (Svensson 2006).

Conclusion

This book attempted a detailed review and synthesis of literature on Corruption as well as its causes, effects, measurement and control and in the process, put forth the concept of Corruptance in organizations and suggested the development of a Corruptance Index, which could be a useful tool to assess organizations' vulnerability to corruption. We started with several questions such as "Is it possible to derive from theory, certain variables from the structure, and environment of organizations, which can point towards the organization's corruption vulnerability or anticorruption preparedness?" "*Is it possible to assess an organization's vulnerability to corruption?; and, "Is it possible to grade and compare multiple organizations' relative preparedness against corruption?*" We have shown through the term Corruptance (the assessed vulnerability of the systems and procedures of the organization to the risk of corruption; or lack of preparedness of the systems and procedures to the threat of internal corrupt activity), how the above questions can be answered. For readers in India we have incorporated a chapter on the anti-corruption scenario in India, as one of the World's fastest growing economies struggling to put in systems and processes in its globalizing organizations. We hope that this effort makes a significant contribution to the discussion on one of the most relevant and pressing issues studied world-wide today, Corruption, and we hope to take this discussion forward in the coming days.

An Afterword:
Presenting The Tenets of Integrity
for Public Servants

*

In the years that were spent researching in this domain, several well-meaning pieces of advice were received towards how to add more value to the possible outcome of a book. The most interesting and perhaps most relevant suggestion was to compile and place before the reader a set of basic tenets for Public Integrity. Public Integrity, of course, refers to the behavioural and ethical values that any Public Servant needs to have and what the public in a democracy may expect from a Public Servant. I am aware that with such an attempt, we are moving out from the realm of objective academic research and discourse into an area of social commentary and a normative, advisory role, though this is also based on and derived from our academic exercise described in the earlier pages of this book. Further, we mentioned at the beginning of the book, a pressing need for an ex-ante, preventive and diagnostic look at corruption, which presupposes that there are some such tenets or principles available in literature. Having justified this last section in this manner, we are presenting this section as an Afterword, which is, in no way, an afterthought.

*

In his ground-breaking book, *Public Integrity* (2001), J. Patrick Dobel has described and analysed the elements that constitute integrity in public office. Dobel addresses such issues as when to resign and when to stay in office, mainly in the context of a liberal democracy like the USA. He has applied not only moral theory but also the insights of history, organizational theory, and psychology in his analysis. Dobel has put personal responsibility at the centre of public morality, examining not just the responsibilities of office but also the role of personal moral commitments and promises. We will see below, there are several other sources from which these principles of Public Integrity can be drawn.

To start with, we need to define who a 'Public Servant' is. We know that all government employees are Public Servants. But, is that all? What about persons working on contract jobs with the government? Non Government Organizations providing different services to various communities/sections of the public? Privately owned organizations providing public services like retail shops, telecommunication services, transportation and a variety of other products and services? Those working for a Government Organization but not drawing any pay? They are also handling public money, public trust and generating their own incomes from this. Do they also not have similar moral and social responsibilities?

The Prevention of Corruption Act of the Government of India (1988) defines 'public servant, as persons falling under any of twelve sub clauses, whether appointed or not. These twelve sub clauses include persons drawing pay, fees or commission from Government or local authority or Corporation, body, Judges, arbitrators, cooperative societies, Commissions, Boards etc. for performance of any public duty. Some other laws include even persons paid for by non-governmental or private organizations under this ambit. For the purpose of this chapter, since we are talking about an over-arching concept of morality, responsibility and public duty, we will define a Public Servant as any person (appointed or elected) who is compensated by the State (Central/Union Government or any of the States or their organizations) for their services by way of pay, salary, contractual payment, budgetary support, subsidy, aid or any form of support from the State exchequer. We also include here all members of organizations and individuals who are performing a service for the public including selling, buying, hiring, leasing, renting, counselling, consulting, advising, etc. for any products and services; in so far as their dealings with the public are concerned. Also included are those, whether appointed, elected or nominated, carrying out a public duty without drawing any remuneration from the public exchequer. We will now attempt to give a compact set of principles of Public Integrity which, we suggest, should be applicable to all public servants as described above.

The first problem we encountered was this interesting paradox: for a world beleaguered by an apparent lack of integrity of its public servants and organizations (going by the numerous scams and investigations we have discussed elsewhere in this book), there actually seems to be a surfeit of such values spelt out in our literature. From the simple examples of honesty, truthfulness, obedience and loyalty described by Hans Christian Anderson in his fairy tales for children to the timeless values of selfless service, patriotism, fairness and sacrifice embodied in our epics, ancient scriptures and holy texts of various religious, there is indeed, a large list of principles to choose from. For the purpose of this exercise meant *specifically for public servants and the special nature of their work,* we will need to focus on certain specific values from amongst these.

Besides the profusion of ethical values, there is another issue that none of these sources have actually presented an *exhaustive* list of principles applicable for public servants. There is passing mention of the qualities of popular kings or king's courtiers in the stories extolling their virtues or condemning vices. As mentioned in the second chapter of this book, ethics, historically, were often in the eyes of the historian, just as beauty is in the eyes of the beholder. What was considered ethical and just two thousand years ago for a king or a minister or their employees need not hold good today in its entirety. The king's employees of those days served the king, not the people. So the qualities sought for in 'good' government servants were oriented more towards loyalty to the king, honesty for that very purpose, etc. In today's democracy this loyalty is towards the voting public, and public integrity and the related values are also thereby redirected towards this orientation. Further, writings of Aristotle, Plato and even Chanakya suggest that while the King or Leader has to behave in a particular way towards their subjects in the course of their public duties, there are no such expectations from them in their private lives and transactions. This also cannot be as such made applicable to modern public servants. Taking all these into consideration we have decided to rely largely upon these sources given in table below, for laying down on our principles of Public Integrity.

S.No.	The Sources	Contains Comments on...
1	The ancient Epics and scriptures like *Ramayana* (Rishi Valmiki), *Mahabharata* (Rishi Veda Vyasa), *The Holy Bible*, the *Talmud*, the *Quran*, the *Bhagavat Gita*, etc.	Qualities of ideal Kings, Vices to be avoided, Meaning of and need for sacrificing self-interest, importance of generosity, benevolence, concept of *Nishkama Karma* (work without bothering about quid pro quo), etc.
2	Historical Texts and Essays like *Arthashastra* (Chanakya), *Ethics* (Aristotle), *Republic* (Plato), *Rajatarangini* (Kalhana) and writings of Socrates, Archimedes, Pythagoras, etc.	Duties, ethical behaviour for Kings, Ministers, Courtiers: common forms of corruption, treachery, disloyalty, etc.
3	More modern authors and thinkers and their works like *Ethics* (Benedict de Spinoza), *Gitanjali* (Rabindranath Tagore), *The Story of my Experiments with Truth* (Mohandas Karamchand Gandhi), etc.	Ethical values for individuals, commitment to the Nation, need for individuals to be honest and truthful in personal dealings first, then towards the society, etc.
4	Modern Management Theory; Literature from Journal Articles, Books, etc. on social sciences.	Serious academic scrutiny and theorizing on ethical principles.
5	Efforts of Governments and their agencies in countries such as Great Britain (2014), Australia, New Zealand, several Norwegian Countries, Bhutan, South Korea, etc.	Bureaucratic attempts to streamline and present ethics and integrity values for public servants and the people as a whole

Special mention should be made about the commendable efforts of some Governmental Committees. In 1995, The Committee on Standards in Public Life appointed by the British Parliament submitted a set of such principles and subsequently (2014) suggested materials for implementing the same for their government servants from induction onwards. We have drawn from all the above sources.

Here, then, is the list of principles for Public Integrity that we have short listed:

	The Principle	Can also be called...
1	Selflessness	Unselfishness, Generosity, Altruism, Benevolence
2	Integrity	Probity, Uprightness, Wholeness
3	Objectivity	Impartiality, Fairness, Un-prejudiced, Neutrality
4	Accountability	Responsibility, Open to Scrutiny, Liability to the Law
5	Openness	Transparency, Translucency, No secrecy
6	Honesty	Truthfulness, Trustworthiness, Veracity
7	Leadership	Model, Example, Stewardship, Dependability, Guide.

These are selected from the above described profusion of moral values and social norms as seen in literature. Different sources have described the same value in slightly differing terminology, and hence the alternative terms are presented in the third column above. By and large they correspond to dictionary and thesaurus descriptions, but some of them show a marginal overlap in some descriptions. Examples are Integrity/Honesty and Objectivity/Openness, but for the purpose of this book we propose these seven broadly related, yet independent values as out Seven tenets of Public Integrity. Now, what do they translate as, in practice? For short 'one-line' instructions on implementing these principles and for easy dissemination of these tenets in the public domain, we propose the following.

	Principle	One line instruction...
1	Selflessness	Act only in Public Interest
2	Integrity	Be under obligation to NO ONE
3	Objectivity	Take decisions on merit, without discrimination

4	Accountability	Be responsible to Public, hence Open to public scrutiny
5	Openness	Take decisions in a transparent manner
6	Honesty	Be truthful at all times
7	Leadership	Lead by example in public conduct and private life

Finally we would also like to recommend a simple yet memorable mnemonic for making these seven principles easy to remember for everyone. The name we suggest is GANDHI. Mohandas Karamchand Gandhi was the 'Father of the Nation' of India, having propounded the path of *Satyagraha* (seeking of Truth) and *Ahimsa* (Non-Violence), and was responsible for the successful achievement of independence for India from British dominion. Gandhi-ji was also the author of "The Story of My Experiments with Truth" one of the most popular autobiographies ever. We link the name of this legendary figure to our list of Integrity Principles, as follows. (The seven we identified have been arranged within the six letters by including Honesty (Truthfulness) and Openness (transparency) together under H.

The GANDHI-ji Model of Public Integrity

1	G	**Generosity, Selflessness**
2	A	**Accountability, Responsibility**
3	N	**Neutrality, Objectivity**
4	D	**Dependability, Leadership**
5	H	**Honesty, Openness**
6	I	**Integrity, Uprightness**

As a humble contribution to the ongoing discussion for preventing corruption and promoting Integrity in Organizations, we would like to place the above set of principles in front of our readers. Let us discuss!

Kochi
1st September 2016

References

(Tr), S. M. (2007). *Kalhana's Rajatarangini: A chronicle of the Kings of Kashmir.* Srinagar, India: Saujanya Books.

Ackerman, R. W. (1973). How Companies respond to social demands. *Harward University Review*, 88-98.

Agle, B. R. (1999). Who matters as CEOs?An investigation of stakeholder attributes and salience, Corporate Performance and CEO Values. *Academy of Management Journal*, 507-526.

Alford, H. &. (2002). Beyond the Shareholder model of the Firm: Working Toward the common good of a business. In S. A. eds), *Rethinking the purpose of business: Interdisciplinary Essays from the Catholic Social Tradition* (pp. 27-47). Notre Dame: Notre Dame University Press.

Anders, J., & Nuijten, M. (2007). Corruption and the Secret of Law: An Introduction. In J. Anders, & M. (. Nuijten, *Corruption and the Secret of Law: A Legal Anthropological Perspective.* Hampshire, England: Ashgate Publishing.

Andriof J & McIntosh, M. (2001). *Perspectives on Corporate Citizenship.* Sheffield, UK: Greenleaf.

Aquino, K. &. (2002). The self importance of Moral Identity. *Journal of personality and Moral Psychology.*

Argandona, A. (Article first published online: 29 AUG 2003). Corruption: the corporate perspective. *Business Ethics: A European Review*, Volume 10, Issue 2, Article first published online: 29 AUG 2003.

Vinayan Janardhanan

Arlacchi, P. (1989). *Mafiose Ethik und der geist des Kapitalismus: Die unternehmerische Mafia.* Frankfurt /Main: Cooperative Verlag.

Ashforth, B. &. (2003). The Normalization of Corruption in Organizations. *Research in Organizational Behavior.*

Ashforth, B., Gioia, D. A., Robinson, S. L., & Trevino, L. K. (2008). Introduction to Special Topic Forum: Re-viewing Organizational Corruption. *Academy of Management Review*, 670-684.

Ates, Z. &. (2011). Corporate social responsibility in the public service sector: Towards a sustainability balanced scorecard for local public enterprises. *Journal for Public & Nonprofit Services Vol. 34 Issue 3*, 346-360.

Babiak, P. &. (2003). *Snakes in suits: When psychopaths go to work.* New York: Harper Collins.

Bagozzi, R. (1994). Structural Equation Models in Marketing Research: basic Principles. In R. Bagozzi, *Principles of Marketing Research* (pp. 317-385). Oxford: Blackwell.

Banaji, M., & Bazerman, M. C. (2003). How (un)ethical are you? *Harward Business Review.*

Bandura, A. (1986). *Social Foundations of Thought and Action: A social cognitive theory.* Englewood Cliffs. NJ: Prentice-Hall.

Bandura, A. (1999). Moral Disengagement in the Perpetration of Inhumanities. *Personality and Social Psychology Review.*

Bardhan, P. (2006). The Economist's Approach to the Problem of Corruption. *World Development*, Vol. 34, No. 2, pp. 341–348.

Barnard, C. I. (1938). The Economy of Incentives. In C. Barnard, *The Functions of the Executive.* Cambridge, Massacheussets: Harward University press.

Bartels, L. K., Harrick, E., & Strickland, K. M. (1998). The relationship between ethical climate and ethical problems within human resource management. *Journal of Business Ethics*, 799-804.

Beeri, I., Dayan, R., Vigoda-Gadot, E., & Werner, S. B. (2013). Advancing Ethics in Public organizations: The impact of an Ethics program on employees' perceptions and behaviours in a regional council. *Journal of Business Ethics.*

Bennett, R. a. (2000). Development of a measure of workplace deviance. *Journal of Applied Psychology*, 349-60.

122

Bhaya, H. (1990). Management efficiency in private and public sectors in India. In J. Heath, *Public Enterprise at the Crossroads.* London: Routledge.

Blackburn, K. a. (2008). Corruption, development and demography. *Economics of Governance*, 341-62.

Bollen, K. (1984). Multiple Indicators:Internal Consistency of No necessary Relationship? *Quality and Quantity*, 377-385.

Brasz, H. (1970). The Sociology of Corruption. In A.J.Heidenheimer(Ed), *Political Corruption:Readings in Comparative Analysis.* New York: Holt,Reinhart&Winston.

Brief, A., & Buttram, R. &. (2001). Collective Corruption in the Corporate world: Toward a process model. In M. (. Ed), *Groups at Work: Theory and Research.* Mahwah, NJ: Lawrence Erlbaum Associates.

Brown, M., & Trevino, L. &. (2005). Ethical leadership: A social learning perspective for construct development and testing. *Organizational Behavior and Human Decision Processes.*

Budhwar, P. &. (2009). Future research on human resource management systems in Asia. *Asia Pacific Journal of Management*, 197-218.

Butterfield, K., Trevino, L., & Weaver, G. (2000). Moral Awareness in Business Organizations: Influences of Issue Related and social context factors. *Human Relations.*

Carroll, A. (1999). Corporate Social Responsibility:Evolution of a Definitional Construct. *Business and Society*, 268-295.

Chandler, A. (1993). Organizational Capabilities and Industrial restructuring. *Journal of Comparative Economics.*

Clinard, M. (1990). *Corporate Corruption:The abuse of Power.* New York: Praeger.

Cohen, A. (2016). Are they among us? A conceptual framework of the relationship between the dark triad personality and counterproductive work behaviors. *Human Resource Management Review*, 69–85.

Cohen, A. (March 2016). Are they among us? A conceptual framework of the relationship between the dark triad personality and counterproductive work behaviors (CWBs). *Human Resource Management Review.*, 69-85.

Collins, D. (2000). The quest to improve the human condition: The first 1500 articles published in Journal of Business Ethics. *Journal of Business Ethics*, 1-72.

D, V. (1986). The study of social Issues in Management: A critical appraisal. *California Management Review*, 142-152.

Daley, J., harrick, E., Schaefer, D., & Sullivan, D. S. (1996,15). HR's View of ethics in the work place: Are the barbarians at the gate?. *Journal of Business Ethics*, 273-285.

Davis, K. (1960). Can business afford to ignore Corporate Social Responsibility? *California Management Review*, 70-76.

Davis, K. (1967). Understanding the Social Responsibility Puzzle. *Business Horizons*, 45-51.

Deloitte. (2008). *Taking the Reins: HR's opportunity to play a leadership role in governance, risk management and compliance.* Midtown: Manhattan: Deloitte Consulting.

Diamantopoulos, A. &. (2001). Index Construction with Formative Indicators: An alternative to scale development. *Journal of Marketing Research*, 269-277.

Dichtl, E. a.-G. (1986). Country Risk Ratings. *Management Internatinal Review*, 4 - 11.

Donaldson, T. a. (1995). the stakeholder theory of the corporation: Concepts, Evidence and Implications. *Academy of management Review*, 65-91.

Dunfee, D. T. (1994). Towards a unified conception of Business ethics: integrative social contracts theory. *Academy of Management Review*, 252-284.

Dunfee, D. T. (1999). *Ties that Bind: Asocial contracts approach to Business Ethics.* Boston: Harward Business School Press.

Dwyer, S., & Tan, C. M. (2014). Hits and Runs: Determinants of the cross-country variation in the severity of impact from the 2008-09 financial crisis. *In Journal of Macroeconomics*.

Eby, L. T. (1998). The impact of taking an ethical approach to employee dismissal during corporate restructuring. *Journal of Business Ethics*, 1253-1264.

Eisenberg, N. (2000). Emotion, regulation and Moral Development. *Annual Review of Psychology*.

Engels, J., Fahrmeir, A., & & Nutzenadel, A. (. (2009). *Geld, Gesschenke, Politik: Korruption im neuzeitlichen Europa.* Munchen: Oldenberg Verlag.

Ermann, M. &. (2001). *Corporate and Governmental Deviance: Problems of Organizational Behaviour in Contemporary Society.* New York: Oxford University Press.

Evan, W. M. (1988). A stakeholder theory of the modern corporation: Kantian Capitalism. In T. B. eds), *Ethical Theory and Business* (pp. 75-93). Englewood Cliffs: Prentice Hall.

Everett, J. N. (2006). The global fight against corruption: a Foucaultian, virtues- ethics framing. *Journal of Business Ethics,* 65, 1–12.

Fein, E. &. (2014). Review and shortcomings of literature on corruption in organizations in offering a multi-faceted and integrative understanding of the phenomenon. *Behavioral Development Bulletin of American Psychological Association,* 67-77.

Fornell, C. &. (1982). AComparative Analysis of two Structural Equation models: LISREL and PLS Applied to Market Data. In *A Second Generation of Multivariate Analysis Vil. 1* (pp. 289-324). New York: Praeger.

Fornell, C. a. (1994). Partial Least Squares. In R. B. (ed), *Advanced Methods of Marketing Research* (pp. 52 - 78). Oxford: Blackwell.

Fornell, C. R. (1991). Direct Regression, Reverse Regression and Covariance Structure Analysis. *Marketing Letters,* 52 - 78.

Frederick, W. C. (1978). From CSR1 to CSR2: The maturing of Business and Society Thought. *Working Paper No 279.* Graduate School of Business, University of Pittsburgh.

Freeman, R. E. (1984). *Strategic Management: A Stakeholder Approach.* Boston: Pitman.

Freeman, R. E. (1994). The politics of Stakeholder theory: Some future directions. *Business Ethics Quarterly,* 409-429.

Freeman, R. E. (2002). Stakeholder Theory: A Libertarian Defence. *Business Ethics Quarterly,* 331-349.

Freisitzer, K. (1981). Gesellschaftliche Bedingungen der Korruption-Versuch einer verhaltenswissenschaftlichen Deutung. In C. (. Bru"nner, *Korruption und Kontrolle* (pp. S.151–163). Wien.

Friedman, M. (1970, September 13). The Social Responsibility of Business is to increase its profits. *New York Times Magazine,* pp. 122,126.

Fritzen, S. A. (2007). Crafting performance measurement systems to reduce corruption risks in complex organizations: The case of the World Bank. *Measuring Business Excellence.*

Frost, A. &. (2006). How, when and why bad apples spoil the barrel: Negative group members and disfunctional groups. *Research in Organizational Behaviour.*

Garriga, E. &. (2004). Corporate Social Responsibility Theories: Mapping the Territory. *Journal of Business ethics,* 51-71.

Gautam, R. &. (2010). Corporate Social Responsibility Practices in India: A study of Top 500 companies. *Global Business and Management Research: An International Journal,* 41-56.

Gauthier, J. (2008). The universal declaration of ethical principles for psychologists: third draft. *International Association of Applied Psychology,* 67-72.

Gellerman, S. (1986). Why 'good' managers make bad ethical choices. *Harward Business Review.*

Giacalone, R., & Riordan, C. &. (1997). Employee sabotage:Toward a Practitioner-Scholar understanding. In R. &. Giacalone, *Antisocial Behaviour in Organizations.* Thousand Oaks, CA: Sage.

Gibbs, J. P. (1975). *Crime, Punishment, and Deterrence.* New York: Elsevier.

Gioia, D. (2003b). Teaching Teachers to Teach Corporate Governance. *Journal of Management and Governance.*

Gioia, D. (2003b). Teaching Teachers to Teach Corporate Governance. *Journal of Management and Governance.*

Gioia, D. A. (2003). Business organization as instrument of societal responsibility. *Organization,* 435-438.

Gladwin, T. N. (1995). Shifting Paradigms for Sustainable Development: Implications for Management Theory and Research. *Academy of Management Review,* 874-904.

Greenberg, J. (1998). The cognitive geometry of employee theft: Negotiating 'the line' between taking and stealing. In A. O.-K. R.W.Griffin, *Dysfunctional Behavior in Organizations: Nonviolent Dysfunctional Behavior.* Stamford,CT: JAI Press.

Greenwood, M. R. (2002). Ethics and HRM: A Review and Conceptual Analysis. *Journal of Business Ethics,* 261-268.

Greenwood, M. R. (2013). Ethical Analysis of HRM: A Review and Research Agenda. *Journal of Business Ethics*, 355-366.

Greve, H. R., Palmer, D., & Pozner, J. (2010,). Organizations Gone Wild:The Causes, Processes, and Consequences of Organizational Misconduct. *The Academy of Management Annals Vol. 4, No. 1*, 53–107.

Hettige, H. M. (n.d.). IPPS: The Industrial Pollution Projection.

Hindmoor, A., & McConnell, A. (Oct2013). Why Didn't They See It Coming? Warning Signs, Acceptable Risks and the Global Financial Crisis. *Political Studies, Vol. 61 Issue 3*, 543-560.

Hodgson, G. M. (2007). The Economics of Corruption and the Corruption of Economics: An Institutionalist Perspective. *Journal of Economic Issues*.

Hofstede, G. (2003). *Culture's consequences, comparing values behaviors, institutions and organizations across nations.* Newbury Park: Sage.

India, G. o. (2013, September). *Ministry of Corporate Affairs.* Retrieved from mica. gov.in: http://www.mica.gov.in/Ministry/pdfCompanies act 2013.pdf

Jackson, R., & Wood, C. M. (2013). The Dissolution of Ethical Decision-Making in Organizations:A Comprehensive Review and Model. *Journal of Business Ethics*, 233-250.

Jacobs, G., & Belschak, F. D. (2014). (Un)Ethical Behavior and Performance Appraisal: The Role of Affect, Support, and Organizational Justice. *Journal of Business Ethics*, 63-76.

Jalan, B. (1991). *India's Economic crisis: The Way Ahead.* New Delhi: Oxford University Press.

Jensen, M. C. (2000). Value Maximization, Stakeholder Theory and the Corporate Objective Function. In M. B. Eds., *Breaking the code of Change* (pp. 37-58). Boston: Harward Business School Press.

Johnston, M. (2005). Keeping the answers, changing the questions: Corruption Definitions revisited. In U. von Alemann, *Dimensionen Politischer Korruption Beltrage Zum Stan derInternationalen forschung* (pp. 61-76). Weisbaden: VS.

Jones, D. &. (2014). Introducing the short dark triad (SD3). A brief measure of dark personality traits.. *Assessment*, 28–41.

Jones, T. M. (1980). Corporate Social Responsibility revisited, redefined. *California Management Review*, 59-67.

Jourdain, R. &. (2003). *Analysing the Public Procurement Process to identify and eliminate risks of corruption..* Kuala Lampur:: Asian Development Bank.

Judge, W., Mc Natt, D., & & Xu, W. (2011). The antecedents and effects of national corruption: A meta-analysis. *Journal of World Business,* 93–103.

Kaku, R. (1997). The path of Kyosei. *Harward Business Review,* 55-62.

Kaufmann, D. a. (2007). *On measuring governance: framing issues for debate. Issues paper for Round Table on Measuring Governance.* Washington DC: World bank Institute.

Kaufmann, D. K. (2008). *Governance matters: Governance Indicators for 1998-2006.* www.worldbank.org/wbi/governance/pubs/govmatters2007.htm.

Kelloway, E. B. (n.d.). *Handbook of Workplace Violence.* Thousand Oaks, CA:: Sage.

Khan, M. (1996). A typology of Corrupt Transactions in Developing Countries. *IDS Bulletin.*

Kohlberg, L. (1969). *Stage and Sequence: The cognitive development approach to socialization.* Chicago: Rand McNally.

Kopf, J., & Carnevale, J. &. (n.d.). Globalism, Capitalism and Negative Externalities: Anecdotes of Bad Behavior. *The Journal of Global Business Issues – Volume 7 Issue 2.*

KPMG,2008. Fraud Survey 2008. (2009). *http://www.kpmg.com.au.* Retrieved August 22, 2014, from www.kpmg.com.au: http://www.kpmg.com. au/Portals/0/Fraud%20Survey%202008.pdf

KPMG,2013. (2013). *A Survey of fraud, bribery and corruption in Australia and New Zealand 2012.* Retrieved April 10, 2014, from http://www.kpmg.com: http://www.kpmg.com/au/en/issuesandinsights/articlespublications/fraudsurvey/pages/fraud-bribery-corruption-survey-2012.aspx

L.K.Jha, & K.N.Jha. (1998). Chanakya the pioneer economist of the world. *International Journal of Social Economics,* 267-282.

Lambsdorff, J. (2008). *The institutional economics of corruption and reform.* London: Cambridge University Press.

Lang, M., & Schmidt, P. G. (2015). The Early Warnings of Banking Crises; Interaction of Broad Liquidity and Demand Deposits. *Journal of International Money and Finance.*

Lange, D. (2008). A MULTIDIMENSIONAL CONCEPTUALIZATION. *Academy of Mnagement Review,* 710-729.

Lankoski, L. (2009). Differential economic impacts of corporate responsibility issues. *Business & Society,* 206-224.

Lanyon, R. &. (2004). Validity and reliability of a pre-employment screening test: The counter-productive behaviour index. *Journal of Business and Psychology.*

Lefkowitz, J. (2009). Individual and organizational antecedents of misconduct in organizations: what do we (believe that we) know, and on what bases do we (believe that we) know it? In R. J. Eds), *Research Companion to Corruption in Organizations* (pp. 60-91). Massachusetts: Edward Elgar Publishing Limited.

Lewin, K. (1939). Field theory and experiment in social psychology: concepts and methods. *American Journal of Sociology,* 44, 868-96.

Lewis, G. (2004). Violence at work: causes and prevention. In J. T. (eds).

Lipset S. M.& Lenz, G. (2000). Corruption, Culture and Markets. In L. E. Harrison, & S. P. and Huntington, *Culture matters: How Values Shape Human Progress* (pp. 112-125). New York: Basic Books.

Lo'pez, J. A., & Santos, J. M. (2014). Does Corruption Have Social Roots? The Role of Culture and Social Capital. *Journal of Business Ethics,* 697-708.

Lodgson, W. D. (2002). Business Citizenship: From individuals to organizations. *Business ethics Quarterly,* 59-94.

Luo, Y. (2002). Corruption and organziation in Asian management systems. *Asia Pacific Journal of Management;,* 405-422.

Mabbett, I. (1964). The Date of Arthashastra. *Journal of the American Oriental Society,* 162-169.

MacCallum, R. a. (1993). The Use of Causal Indicators in Covariance Structure Models: Some Practical Issues. *Psychological Bulletin,* 533 - 541.

Mahon, W. a. (1994). Towards a substantive defenition of the Corporate issue Construct: A review and Synthesis of literature. *Business and Society,* 293-311.

Majumdar, S. (1998). Assessing Comparative Efficiency of the State-Owned Mixed and Private sectors in Indian Industry. *Public Choice,* 1-24.

Mani, M., & Wheeler, D. (1997). IN SEARCH OF POLLUTION HAVENS? *OECDOECD Conference on FDI and the Environment*. The Hague: World Bank.

Marcus, B. &. (2004). Anticedents of counterproductive work-place behaviour: A general perspective. *Journal of Applied Psychology*.

Maslow, A. (1954). *Motivation and Personality*. New York: Harper.

Matten, D., & Crane, A. (2004, (IN PRESS)). Corporate Citizenship: Towards an extended theoretical conceptualization. *Academy of Management Review*.

Mauss, M. (2002). *The Gift: The form and reason for exchange in Archaic societies*. London: Routledge.

Mele, D. (2002). *Not only Stakeholder interests: The firm oriented towards the common good*. Notre Dame: Notre Dame University Press.

Mensah, Y. M. (2014). An Analysis of the Effect of Culture and Religion on Perceived Corruption in a Global Context. *Journal of Business Ethics*, 121:255–282.

Messick, D. &. (1996). Ethical Leadership and the Psychology of Decision making. *Sloan Management Review*.

Meyer, M. R. (2011). Human Resources Risk Management: Governing people risks for improved performance. *SA Journal of Human Resource Management*, 12 pages.

The University of Michigan, (1967). The Orissa Historical Research Journal, Volume 16, Issues 1-3. Orissa, India: Superintendent of Research and Museum.

Misangyi, V. F., Weaver, G. R., & Elms, H. (2008). Ending Corruption: The interplay among institutional logics, resources and institutional entrepreneurs. *Academy of Management Review*, 750–770.

Mitchell, R., & Wood, A. (1997). Toward a theory of stakeholder identification and salience: Defining the principle of who and what really counts. *Academy of Management Review*, 853-886.

Moore, D., Tetlock, P., & Tanlu, l. &. (2006). Conflicts of interest and the case of auditor independence: Moral seduction and strategic issue cycling. *Academy of Management Review*.

Mossholder, K. W., Giles, W. F., & Wesolowski, a. M. (1991). Information Privacy and Performance Appraisal: An examination of employee perceptions and reactions. *Journal of Business Ethics*, 151-156.

Mukheree, K. (2013). DELIVERY OF MANDATED CSR: Sensemaking process of Managers. *Under print.*

Mulgan, R. (2012). Aristotle on Legality and Corruption. In B. H. Manuhuia Barcham, *Corruption: Expanding the Focus* (p. Chapter 2). Australian National University, ANU E-press.

Murray, K. B. (1986). strategic management of the Socially Responsible firm:integrating Management and Marketing Theory. *Academy of Management review*, 815-828.

Naidoo, R. (2002). *Corporate Governance: An essential guide for South Africon Companies.* Cape Town: Double Storey.

Nations, U. (1999). *Global Compact.* Retrieved from www.unglobalcompact. org

Neal M. Ashkanasy, C. P. (01-Dec-2010). *The Handbook of Organizational Culture and Climate.* SAGE Publications, - Business & Economics.

Nisbett, R. R. (1980). *Human Inference: Strategirs and shortcomings of Social Judgement.* Englewood Cliffs, NJ.: Prentice-Hall.

North, C. M., Orman, W. H., & Gwin, C. R. (August 2013). Religion, Corruption, and the Rule of Law. *Journal of Money, Credit and Banking*, Vol. 45, No. 5, P757-779.

Nye, J. (1967). Corruption and Political development:A cost - benefit analysis. *American Political Science Review.*

O'Hara, P. A. (Vol. XLVIII No. 2 June 2014). Political Economy of Systemic and Micro-Corruption throughout the World. *Journal of Economic issues*, 279-307.

O'Boyle, E. F. (2011).). Bad apples or bad barrels: An examination of group- and organizational-level effects in the study of counterproductive work behavior. *Group & Organization Management*, 39–69.

O'Boyle, E. J. (2012).. A meta-analysis of the dark triad and work behavior: A social exchange perspective.. *Journal of Applied Psychology*, 557–579.

Okpara, J. O. (2008). man Resource Management practices in a transition economy: Challenges and prospects. *Management Research News.*

Paldam, M. (2002). The cross-country pattern of corruption: Economics culture and the seesaw dynamics. *European Journal of Political Economy*, 18, 215–240.

Partners in Change. (2013, November). *PIC Website.* Retrieved from www. picindia.org: www.picindia.org

Petrick, J. A. (2012). Enhancing Ethical U.S. HRM Education and Practice: Integrity Capacity and HRM Professionalism. *SAM Advanced Management Journal*, 42-60.

Phillips, R. A. (2003). What Stakeholder Theory is Not. *Business Ethics Quarterly*, 479-502.

Porter, M. M. (2002). The Competitive advantage of Corporate Philanthropy. *Harward Business Review*, 56-69.

Post, P. L. (1975). *Private Management and Public Policy: The principle of Public Responsibility*. Englewood Cliffs,NJ: Prentice Hall.

Post, P. L. (1981). Private Management and Public Policy. *California management Review*, 56-63.

Price-Waterhouse Coopers. (2001 January). *The Opacity Index*. Price Waterhouse Coopers.

Purcell, A. J. (2014). Corruption and misconduct: A behavioural reflection from investigative reports into local Government. *Journal of Business Systems, Governance and Ethics,* Vol 9, No 1.

Rabl, T. &. (2008). Understanding Corruption in Organizations- Development and Empirical Assessment of an Action model. *Journal of Business Ethics*.

Rabl, T. (2011). The Impact of Situational Influences on Corruption in Organizations. *Journal of Business Ethics*.

Reed, A. I. (2003). Moral Identity and the expanding circle of moral regard toward out-groups. *Journal of Personality and Social Psychology*.

Reynolds, S. (2006). Moral awareness and ethical predispositions:Investigating the role of individual differences in the recognition of moral issues. *Journal of Applied Psychology*.

Rhodes, C. &. (2012). Agonism and the Possibilities of Ethics for HRM. *Journal of Business Ethics*, 49-59.

Richter, H. E. (1989). *Die hohe kunst der korruption: Erkenntnisse eines politik-berators*. Hamburg: Heyne Verlag.

Robinson, S. &. (1998). Constructiong the reality of Normative Behaviour:The use of neutralization strategies by organizational deviants. In A. O.-K. R.W.Griffin, *Disfunctional Behaviour in Organizations: Violent and Deviant Behaviour*. Stamford,CT: JAI Press.

Robinson, S. a. (1995). A typology of deviant workplace behaviors: a multidimensional scaling study. *Academy of Management Journal*, 555-72.

Robinson, S. O.-K. (1998). Monkey see, Monkey do: The influence of work groups on antisocial behaviour of employees. *Academy of Management Journal.*

Robison, D. (1988). Industrial Pollution Abatement: The Impact on the Balance of Trade. *Canadian Journal of Economics,* 701-706.

Rowley, T. J. (1997). Moving beyond Dyadic Ties: A network theory of stakeholder influences. *Academy of Management Review,* 887-911.

Rubin, P. H. (1990). *Managing Business Transactions.* New York: Free Press.

Rugemer, W. (1996). Wirtschaften ohne Korruption. *Fischer-Taschenbuch-Verlag, Frankfurt am Main.*

Ryan, L. V. (2006). Current Ethical Issues in Polish HRM. *Journal of Business Ethics,* 273-290.

Schweitzer, M., & Ordonez, L. D. (2004). Goal Setting as a motivator of unethical behaviour. *Academy of Management Journal.*

Scott, C. (1972). *Comparative political corruption.* Englewood Cliffs: Prentice Hall.

Senturia, J. (1930). Corruption, Political. *Encyclopedia of the Social Sciences, Vol 4,* 448-452.

Sethi, S. P. (1975). Dimensions of Corporate Social Performance: An analytical framework. *California Management Review,* 58-65.

Shadnam, M. &. (2011). Understanding Widespread Misconduct in Organizations: An Institutional Theory of Moral Collapse. *Business Ethics Quarterly,* 379-407.

Smith, S. &. (2013). Psychopathy in the workplace: The knowns and unknowns.. *Aggression and Violent Behavior, 18,* 204–218.

Sohail, M. &. (2008; 134(9),). Accountability to prevent corruption in Construction projects.. *Journal of Construction Engineering Management.,* 729–38.

Soreide, T. (2002:1). *Corruption in Public Procurement: Causes, Consquences and Cures.* Bergen: CMI.

Spain, S. H. (2014).. The dark side of personality at work.. *Journal of Organizational Behavior,* S41–S60.

Stilwell, R. C. (1991). *Packaging for the Environment: A. Ž. Partnership for Progress.* New York: A. D. Little, Inc.

Stretton, S. (1994). Maslow and the Modern Public Servant:A lateral approach to performance and integrity in the public sector work environment. *Australian Journal of Public Administration*.

Svensson, J. (2005). Eight Questions about Corruption. *American Economic Association's Journal of Economic Perspectives*, 19-42.

Swanson, D. L. (1995). Addressing a theoretical problem by Reorienting the Corporate Social Performance Model. *Academy of Management Review*, 43-64.

Tabish, S. J. (2011). Analysis and Evaluation of Irregularities in Public Procurement in India.. *Construction Management and Economics.*, 261-274.

Temin, P. (1997). Is it Kosher to talk about culture? *Journal of Economic History*, 57(2), 267–287.

Thai, K... (2008). *International Handbook of Public procurement.*. New York:: CRC Press, Taylor and Francis Group.

Tittle, C. R. (1980). *Sanctions and Social Deviance: TheQuestion of Deterrence.* New York: Praeger.

Tobey, J. (1990). The Effects of Domestic Environmental Policies on Patterns of World Trade: An Empirical Test. *Kyklos*, 191-209.

Tobey, J. (1990). The Effects of Domestic Environmental Policies on Patterns of World Trade: An Empirical Test. *Kyklos*, 191-209.

Toffler, B. (. (2003). *Final Accounting: Ambition, Greed and the fall of Arthur Anderses.* New York: Broadway Books.

Tonnies, F. (1947). *Comunidad y sociedad.* Buenos Aires: Losada.

Treisman, D. (2000). The causes of corruption: A cross-national study.. *Journal of Public Economics*, 73, 399–457.

Trevino, L. K. (1986). Ethical Decision making in organizations: A person-situation interactionist model. *Academy of Management Review*.

Trevino, L. K. (1990). Bad Apples in Bad Barrels:A causal analysis of ethical decision making behaviour. *Journal of Applied Psychology*.

Trevino, L., & Butterfield, K. &. (1998). The ethical context in organizations: Influences on employee attitudes and behaviors. *Business Ethics Quarterly*.

Trevino, L., Weaver, G., & Gibson, D. &. (1999). Managing ethics and legal compliance: What works and what hurts. *California Management Review*.

Turner, M., Imbaruddin, A., & Sutiono, W. (2009). Human Resource Management: The Forgotten Dimension Of Decentralisation In Indonesia. *Bulletin of Indonesian Economic Studies*, 231-249.

Umphress, E., & Barsky, A. &. (2005). Be careful what you wish for:Goal setting, Procedural justice and ethical behaviour at work. *Academy of Management, Honolulu.* Honolulu.

Unit, E. I. (1996). *Global EIU Market Indexes.* London: Economist Intelligence Unit.

Varadarajan, P., & Menon, A. (1988). Cause Related Marketing: A coalignment of strategic markeeting and corporate philanthropy. *Journal of Marketing*, 58-58.

Vardi, Y. a. (2004). *Misbehavior in Organizations: Theory, Research and Management.* Lawrence Erlbaum Associates: Mahwah,NJ.

Vaughn, D. (1999). The dark side of organizations: mistake, misconduct, and disaster. *Annual Review of Sociology*, 271-303.

Veit, E. T. (1996). Ethics Violations: A survey of investment analysts. *Journal of Business Ethics*, 1287-1297.

Victor, B. &. (1988). The organizational Bases of Ethical work climates. *Administrative Science Quarterly.*

Volkov, V. (2000). Patrimonialism versus Rational Bureaucracy: On the Historical Relativity of Corruption. In S. e. Lovell, *Negotiating Reciprocity from the early modern period to the 1990s* (pp. 35-47). London: Palgrave Macmillan.

Voslensky, M. (1987). *Nomenklatura: The Soviet Ruling Clastt.* New York: Doubleday.

Wartick, S. a. (1986). The evolution of Corporate Social Performance Model. *Academy of Management Review*, 758-769.

Weaver, G. (2006). Virtue in organizations: Moral identity as a foundation for moral agency. *Organization Studies.*

Weaver, G., Trevino, L., & & Cochran, P. (1999). Integrated and Decoupled Corporate Social Perfoemance: Management Commitments, External Pressures and Corporate Ethics Practices. *Academy of Management Journal.*

Weber, J. &. (2001). Investigating Influences on managers' moral reasoning: The impact of context and personal and organizational factors. *Business and Society.*

Werhane P.H.. (1999). Moral imagination and Management Decision Making. New York: Oxford University press.

Wheeler, S. W. (1988). White Collar crimes and Criminals. *American Criminal Law Review.*

Wilhelm, P. (2002: 35). International validation of the corruption perceptions index. *Journal of Business ethics*, 177–189.

Wood, D. J. (1991 b). Corporate Social Performance Revisited. *Academy of Management Review*, 691-718.

Wright, P. M. (1994). Human resources and sustained competitive advantage: A resource-based perspective. *International Journal of Human Resource Management*, 5 (2) 301–326.

Wright, P. M., & Gardner, T. M. (2003). The impact of HR practices on the performance of business units. *Human Resource Management Journal*, Vol 13 No 3, pages 21-36.

Wright, P. M., Dunford, B. B., & A., &. S. (2001). Human resources and the resource based view of the firm. *Journal of Management*, 27; 701–721.

Zimbardo, P. (2004). *A situationist Perspective of the Psychology of Evil:Understanding how good people are transformed into perpetrators.* New York: Guilford Press.